From School Administrator to School Leader

Learn how to become a leader who truly empowers and inspires others. This practical book shows you how to move from being a manager or administrator who simply gets things done to a leader who motivates others to succeed, creating a more positive work environment. The book covers 15 keys to success that can be used by those in any type of leadership position, from superintendent to principal to department chair or teacher-leader.

You'll discover how to:

- determine your own leadership style;
- develop your strengths;
- develop those you lead;
- be a leader, not just a manager;
- find your voice;
- influence school culture;
- be accountable to those you lead;
- communicate effectively;
- lead with EQ vs. IQ;
- be flexible, adaptable, and creative;
- respond effectively to crisis;
- and much more!

Each chapter provides a variety of strategies for building a particular skill. It also features interviews with well-known leaders from different fields. These experts offer advice that will teach and inspire you as you learn to maximize your own leadership potential.

Dr. Brad Johnson is an international speaker in the field of education. He has spent over 20 years in the education field and currently teaches graduate courses in leadership.

Dr. Julie Sessions has worked in education for 21 years. She is currently a curriculum coordinator at Porter-Gaud Lower School in Charleston, South Carolina.

Other Eye On Education Books Available from Routledge
(www.routledge.com/eyeoneducation)

What Schools Don't Teach:
20 Ways to Help Students Excel in School and Life
Brad Johnson and Julie Sessions

What Teachers Can Learn from Sports Coaches
Nathan Barber

Inquiry and Innovation in the Classroom:
Using 20% Time, Genius Hour, and PBL to Drive Student Success
A. J. Juliani

What Great Principals Do Differently:
Eighteen Things That Matter Most, Second Edition
Todd Whitaker

What Great Teachers Do Differently:
Seventeen Things That Matter Most, Second Edition
Todd Whitaker

Leading School Change:
9 Strategies to Bring Everybody on Board
Todd Whitaker

Motivating & Inspiring Teachers:
The Educator's Guide to Building Staff Morale, Second Edition
Todd Whitaker, Beth Whitaker, and Dale Lumpa

Dealing with Difficult Teachers, Third Edition
Todd Whitaker

High Impact Leadership of High Impact Teachers
Pamela Salazar

Lead On!
Motivational Lessons for School Leaders
Pete Hall

From School Administrator to School Leader

15 Keys to Maximizing Your Leadership Potential

Brad Johnson and Julie Sessions

Taylor & Francis Group
NEW YORK AND LONDON

First published 2016
by Routledge
711 Third Avenue, New York, NY 10017

and by Routledge
2 Park Square, Milton Park, Abingdon, Oxon, OX14 4RN

Routledge is an imprint of the Taylor & Francis Group, an informa business

© 2016 Taylor & Francis

The right of Brad Johnson and Julie Sessions to be identified as author of this work has been asserted by him/her in accordance with sections 77 and 78 of the Copyright, Designs and Patents Act 1988.

All rights reserved. No part of this book may be reprinted or reproduced or utilized in any form or by any electronic, mechanical, or other means, now known or hereafter invented, including photocopying and recording, or in any information storage or retrieval system, without permission in writing from the publishers.

Trademark notice: Product or corporate names may be trademarks or registered trademarks, and are used only for identification and explanation without intent to infringe.

Library of Congress Cataloging in Publication Data
Johnson, Brad, 1969-
From school administrator to school leader : 15 keys to maximizing your leadership potential / by Brad Johnson and Julie Sessions.
pages cm
Includes bibliographical references.
1. Educational leadership. 2. School management and organization. 3. School administrators.
I. Sessions, Julie. II. Title.
LB2805.J636 2015
371.2'011–dc23
2015003907

ISBN: 978-1-138-90350-0 (hbk)
ISBN: 978-1-138-90351-7 (pbk)
ISBN: 978-1-315-69687-4 (ebk)

Typeset in Optima
by Cenveo Publisher Services

(Brad Johnson)
For Melody. You inspire, challenge, and push me to excellence every day and for that I am eternally grateful.

(Julie Sessions)
For my husband, Derek, and my two boys, A.J. and Ed. Without their patience, support, and encouragement, it would have never come to fruition.

Contents

Meet the Authors	ix
Leadership Experts	xi
Introduction	1
Key 1: Know Your Own Leadership Style	3
Key 2: Develop Your Strengths	13
Key 3: Develop Those You Lead	23
Key 4: Be a Leader, Not Just a Manager	31
Key 5: Find Your Voice	39
Key 6: Influence School Culture	49
Key 7: Be Accountable to Those You Lead	57
Key 8: Communicate Effectively	67
Key 9: Lead with Wisdom	77
Key 10: Becoming Resilient and Persevering	87
Key 11: Lead with EQ vs. IQ	95
Key 12: Balance Your Personal and Professional Life	103

Key 13: Be Flexible, Adaptable, and Creative 111

Key 14: Respond Effectively to Crisis 119

Key 15: Know When to Seek Help 129

    Epilogue 137

    Sources 141

Meet the Authors

Dr. Brad Johnson is an international speaker in the fields of education and leadership. He is co-author of *What Schools Don't Teach: 20 Ways to Help Students Excel in School and Life*. Dr. Johnson has spent over 20 years in the education field, with experience as a teacher, curriculum director, and administrator. He has written or contributed to numerous articles as an education expert for magazines including *Education World, Education Digest*, and *Huff Post*. He currently teachers graduate-level leadership courses. He also regularly speaks and consults with CEOs and other business executives in the area of leadership. He is represented by multiple speaking bureaus.

Dr. Julie Sessions is co-author of *What Schools Don't Teach: 20 Ways to Help Students Excel in School and Life*. She has played many roles in education throughout her 21 years in public and private schools in the Charleston area. She has taught in grades 2–7, been a curriculum coordinator, chaired grade levels as well as departments, chaired and co-chaired reaccreditation committees. She earned her undergraduate degree in elementary education with a specialty in literature, a Master's degree in reading from The Citadel, and obtained her certification as a reading diagnostician and reading specialist. She earned her doctorate of education in curriculum studies from Georgia Southern. Dr. Sessions currently serves as curriculum coordinator at Porter-Gaud Lower School in Charleston, South Carolina.

For more information about Dr. Johnson, Dr. Sessions, the book, or speaking availability, please visit www.premiereleaders.com

Leadership Experts

The highly effective leaders who agreed to be interviewed for this book are as follows:

Ann Hart, President of the University of Arizona.

Arthur Carmazzi, ranked as one of the Global Top 10 most influential Leadership Gurus, bestselling author of *Identity Intelligence*.

Bobby Bowden, winningest football coach in Division 1 history (FSU)

Bruce Lloyd, Emeritus Professor of Strategic Management at London South Bank University.

Chester Elton, motivational expert, dubbed the Apostle of Appreciation; bestselling author of *The Carrot Principle*.

Christina Parker, Executive Director of GAYC (Georgia Association on Young Children).

Dan Domenech, Executive Director of AASA (American Association of School Administrators).

David Pennington, President of AASA (American Association of School Administrators).

Dianna Booher, Top 21 speakers of 21st Century.

Emmanuel Gobillot, international leadership expert and bestselling author of *The Connected Leader* and *Leader Shift*.

Fawn Germer, leadership and work-life balance expert; author of bestselling books *Pearls* and *Hard Won Wisdom*.

Gina Ikemoto, Executive Director of Research and Policy Development at New Leaders.

Jim Kouzes, A bestselling author, an award-winning speaker, and, according to the *Wall Street Journal*, one of the 12 best executive educators in the United States.

John Baldoni, An internationally recognized executive coach and educator and the author of 12 leadership books published in 10 languages.

John Chubb, President of NAIS (National Association of Independent Schools).

Judy Vredenburgh, Director of Girls Inc.

Kim Zilliox, leadership development expert; founder of 30 by 30.

Mark Strom, An international leadership expert; author of bestselling book *Lead with Wisdom*.

Marshall Goldsmith, one of the Top 10 most influential business thinkers in the world and the top-ranked executive coach; author of bestselling book *Managers as Mentors: Building Partnerships for Learning*.

Marty Zimmerman, GSI, ASC author/speaker/360 feedback leadership coach/leadership development.

Michelle Boyea, Vice President of McKesson Pharmaceuticals.

Mike Abrashoff, Captain of the USS *Benfold*; author of bestselling book *It's Your Ship*.

Mike Krzyzewski, Head Coach, Duke Basketball (men).

Nancy Zimpher, Chancellor of State University of New York.

Phyllis Wise, Chancellor of University of Illinois at Urbana-Champaign.

Rachael Robertson, leadership expert and Antarctica expedition leader.

Sally Helgesen, ranked 15 in world's Top 30 leadership gurus; author of bestselling book *The Female Vision*.

Sam Silverstein, accountability expert; author of bestselling book *No More Excuses*.

Sarah Davis, founder of ReCreate and Strengthsfinder Consultant.

Terry Orr, Director, Future School Leaders Academy.

Travis Bradberry, leading EQ expert and CEO of TalentSmart; author of bestselling book *Emotional Intelligence 2.0*.

# Introduction

You have been named to a leadership position, but do you have the training it takes to be a true leader? Having a leadership title does not mean you have the tools to be an effective leader. The title describes the job you are hired to do. How you handle the job will show if you are a true leader.

Being in a school leadership position, such as an administrator, department chair, grade-level leader, teacher specialist, or any other leadership position, means that the person is qualified for the job. This qualification can be due to degrees earned or a work ethic that allowed the promotion or recommendation. It doesn't necessarily mean the person possesses the skill set to be an effective leader. John Baldoni (Top 10 ranked international leadership expert and author of 11 books) says there is little difference between promotion to an assistant principal or principal than there is a promotion to manager in the business world. He says that typically these individuals have success and expertise in a given area, but they rarely have experience as a leader. In both instances they would be considered novices in their new leadership role. This may be why research suggests that principal turnover rate is as high as 50% within three to five years. Imagine the instability, lack of staff morale, and effect on student achievement when the "leader" of a school changes every three to five years.

Often people, even experienced administrators, don't fully understand the different styles of leadership and rarely know the leadership strengths or talents that they possess. For example, many administrators work within a transactional style of leadership. Transactional leadership is a style of leadership in which the administrator promotes compliance of his/her followers through both rewards and punishments. Administrators feel pressure to make changes quickly and believe they have to lead this way; unfortunately it is the least effective style of leadership. Most effective leaders work within a transformational style of leadership, where they focus on empowering their staff, creating a positive working environment and making decisions that will create long-term success. Travis Bradberry (author of *Emotional Intelligence 2.0*, internationally recognized expert in Leadership EQ) suggests that there are many EQ (Emotional Intelligence) traits that parallel with transformational traits that many leaders lack.

However, the good news is that these traits can be developed. That's where this book comes in. We examine the skill sets and traits that any person put in a leadership position needs to be effective as a leader. We identify 15 keys to maximizing leadership potential, such as learning about leadership styles, understanding the importance of Emotional Intelligence, finding your voice, knowing the difference between managing and leading, having effective communication, balancing your personal and professional lives, and more.

For each key, skill, or trait, we define and examine what it means then we let experts share their views on why it's important to effective leadership. These experts are frontrunners in leadership, from various fields, whom we interviewed for this book. Their insights and advice can be applied to your own school leadership situation and will hopefully inspire you to develop and grow in your role. Next, we give practical ideas and strategies for implementation. Finally, we wrap up the chapters with key points to remember. We hope this book will give you the tools you need to go from administrator to an effective leader.

Know Your Own Leadership Style

"Leadership is the ability to influence those whom you have the capacity to influence."

Brad Johnson

When asked to define leadership, we tend to think more in terms of people or descriptors that we feel make up effective leadership. We don't tend to think of leadership in terms of styles or lenses. However, understanding the different lenses or styles of leadership can significantly improve your leadership effectiveness and help you understand why others lead the way they do.

I (Brad) have taught leadership courses for several years and I regularly speak on leadership. One question I often ask students, and even veteran leaders, is this: "What leadership style do you use more often?" Most people usually look with an inquisitive or sometimes blank stare, or they ask me, "What do you mean?" In my experience, most leaders don't fully understand the various leadership styles and which ones are most effective, and they aren't aware of their own style. It is quite interesting that in the field of education there seems to be little value placed upon teaching leadership itself.

While education has made an effort to adapt to 21st Century learning, leadership has remained relatively unchanged since the industrial revolution. In fact, educational leadership was built upon the transactional (rewards versus punishment) leadership lens that was developed during the industrial revolution. Since leadership influences culture, motivation, morale, and most aspects of school functioning, the fact that it has remained relatively unchanged could be a factor in why there are so many problems in education today.

Therefore this chapter will examine leadership lenses and styles so that you may become aware of what lenses exist and which are most effective, especially in the 21st Century where the assembly-line culture has been replaced. While there are several different leadership lenses, we will focus on four—trait, transactional, transformational, and servant—in an effort to help you better understand which styles are best aligned with effective leadership, creating positive school cultures, and empowering faculties to achieve their greatest potential. Understanding the various leadership lenses, the lens you currently use, and which lenses are most effective can help you become a more successful leader and maximize not only your potential, but also the potential of those you lead.

Style 1: Trait Leader

For centuries, most leaders subscribed to the "Great Man" theory, which stated leaders were born with certain traits or talents which made them great leaders. This leadership lens is known as **trait** leadership style. A trait is something we are born with and examples include physical size, intellect, charisma, humor, and other traits. A good example of this would be the height of most U.S. presidents, which is typically 3 to 4 inches taller than the average of height of a male in the US. **Dan Domenech**, Executive Director of AASA, explained in an interview with us that there are people who are born with certain leadership traits. Think of people who become captain of the football team, president of a class, or other successes without taking a leadership class. As Domenech explained, people with natural leadership traits seem to be more comfortable in leadership roles, and need more *polishing* of skills rather than actual *developing* of skills.

However, Domenech also explained that the majority of leaders aren't born with these traits and thus need to develop leadership skills and qualities through learned behaviors, mentoring, and effective leadership preparation programs. One issue that may arise is that some leaders may assume they have innate leadership skills since they have been placed or promoted into a leadership role, so they assume the decisions they make are sound and correct when in fact they are not. The good news is that, while you may not naturally possess qualities such as high intelligence, charisma, or an extrovert personality, you can still develop into an effective leader.

Style 2: Transactional Leader

The most commonly used leadership lens is the **transactional** lens. This style of leadership is based on the setting of objectives and goals for the followers, as well as the use of either punishments or rewards in order to encourage compliance with these goals. Unfortunately, this is also the least effective style of leadership. When we think of ineffective leaders (and we have all worked for them at some point!), their hallmark was probably a rewards versus punishment style. Transactional leadership is a basic managerial style that focuses on controlling, organizing, and short-term planning. This doesn't mean that transactional leadership is necessarily bad, but that it is insufficient in maximizing the potential of the leader or followers. Some of the key elements include:

- based around power and position
- short-term focused, not focused on long-term success
- behavioralist (rewards vs. punishment)
- efficiency-centered (bottom-line-only focused)
- structure-dependent (thinks inside the box).

The relationship between the leader (boss) and the employee is "I will give you this if you give me that," where the leader controls the rewards, or contingencies. Historically, this has been the "do as I say, or else" leadership style. Transactional leadership style is simple and effective in short-term and non-complex situations, relying on a system of reward and punishment to motivate followers. This style of leadership does not encourage creativity and is not effective in long-range situations in which input from followers is necessary.

While this lens is common in schools, partly because there is such pressure to make quick changes, such as raising test scores, these types of people aren't given time to develop into effective leaders. As **Dr. Terry Orr** points out, "leaders can't *transaction* their way into effective leadership or creating a positive culture for their employees." While not all transactional leaders are ineffective, this is definitely not the most productive or effective leadership style, as it leaves both the leader and followers unfulfilled.

Michelle Boyea suggests that transactional leadership is commonplace in the corporate world as well. As she explained, "I have had many employees who keep in contact with me over the years because I took the time to get to know them. They say most leaders don't know their name or, if they do, that's about all they know about them. They are more focused on productivity than on the person." She said, "It makes me feel good to know that I made a positive impact on their lives because most leaders in the corporate world are simply not memorable."

What a great thought: becoming a leader who is memorable! The following two leadership lenses will help leaders not only become more effective, but hopefully help them become memorable to all they lead.

Style 3: Transformational Leader

Transformational leadership is distinguished from other lenses of leadership by its call for long-term visioning, selfless concern for followers' personal development, and the transformation of followers into leaders and moral agents. However, the primary focus is on some type of change within the organization. In the educational field, transformation can include a focus on raising graduation rates, improving school culture, raising test scores, teacher attrition, or a myriad other issues.

Transformational leaders lead "by example." Tasks are attacked with a hands-on approach. These leaders have a plan for themselves and their followers and do not divert from it. It is an approach that inspires valuable and positive change in its followers, through motivation, increases in morale, and inspiration to achieve at a high level. The transformational leader works to help others to help each other, to look out for each other, to be encouraging and harmonious, and to look out for the group as a whole.

The four major elements of transformational leadership include:

1. **Idealized Influence**—The leader serves as an ideal role model for followers; the leader "walks the talk," and is admired for this.
2. **Inspirational Motivation**—Transformational leaders have the ability to inspire and motivate followers. Combined, these first two "I"s are what constitute the transformational leader's charisma.
3. **Individualized Consideration**—Transformational leaders demonstrate genuine concern for the needs and feelings of followers. This personal attention to each follower is a key element in bringing out their very best efforts.
4. **Intellectual Stimulation**—The leader challenges followers to be innovative and creative. A common misunderstanding is that transformational leaders are "soft," but the truth is that they constantly challenge followers to higher levels of performance.

In education, transformational leaders give others opportunity to provide solutions to problems and let them use their strengths to improve school or district functioning. Transformational leaders don't use rewards and punishment to get something out of someone, but rather develop each individual to reach his or her full potential.

Style 4: Servant Leader

Servant leadership may be the least common, but is in many respects the most effective and enduring leadership style. This style doesn't mean that the leader acts a servant to followers and has no leadership authority, but rather that the leader focuses on encouraging, empowering, and equipping followers to be successful. This lens is often portrayed as an inverted pyramid where the followers are on top of the pyramid rather than the leaders. Some of the key elements of this style include:

- open communication
- providing sufficient resources and training
- enabling and supporting employee growth
- providing a positive work environment
- empowering employees.

While there are several lenses of leadership, most of the experts we interviewed tend to connect with the transformational or servant lens. But one of the issues in education is that novice leaders aren't given much time to develop into these types of leaders. They are expected to produce certain results in a limited amount of time and, if they don't, then someone else is placed in the position. The problem with this type of transactional leadership is that there are no long-term solutions implemented and there is little input from employees. This means no one feels fulfilled in his/her prospective role in the transactional lens.

What the Experts Say

Now that we've examined the basics of leadership lenses, let's spend more time on what some well-known leadership experts have to say about

Key 1

these different styles. These leaders are from a variety of different fields, and their expertise can easily be applied to education and help you improve your practice. Their insights and experiences are revealed in the passages below.

As **Chester Elton**, author of *The Carrot Principle* explains, "servant leadership is the most effective style of leadership in many instances. Leadership is often seen as top down, and they have responsibility and set the tone, but everyone owns the concert. So followers need to have buy in and ownership in the process." Elton shared an example of a business that he works with on how they make sure their employees' satisfaction is a focus. He said, in training films, Hard Rock Café shows their dishwasher rocking out and enjoying his job. As he says, "If the dishwasher gets it, then everyone gets it."

This is why it is so important to build strong relationships with your people. Remember, teachers will teach and lead students the way you lead them. If teachers feel the support needed to succeed in their classrooms, then the students will ultimately benefit. When we think about our best teachers, you will often find that their success can be attributed to administration leading and supporting them. In contrast, teachers who are not feeling supported and led properly by administration will often experience failure within the classroom setting.

Christina Parker, GAYC Executive Director, states:

> Servant leadership is at the heart of everything I do. I love to see people develop and thrive. In my opinion you cannot lead people without loving them. Leadership is nothing more than influence and the ability to obtain followers and being able to inspire them to see beyond what they think their capabilities are. I believe that when you operate out of a servant leadership position and honestly help people grow personally you win their hearts. Loyalty to a leader reaches the highest level when the follower has personally grown through the mentorship of the leader.

Based upon Christina's reflections, it is clear that the goal of servant leadership should be to develop and invest in those around them so much that the team can step forward and the leader steps back as they support the team to be successful. Servant leaders make sure teachers have the tools to implement initiatives, such as professional development, and also take the time to know about their personal lives and, in essence, humanize the leader-follower relationship.

Nancy Zimpher, Chancellor of State University of New York, discussed her experience with transformational leadership in the following interview excerpt:

> When I came to the State University of New York as Chancellor in 2009, we embarked pretty immediately on creating a new strategic plan for our huge system. We knew that it needed to be a dynamic plan—one that felt like it lived and breathed—and would be truly transformational for the system. With 64 colleges and universities of varying types—the most comprehensive system in the nation—we needed to create a plan that would forge a strong identity for the system as a whole, building away from the long-held sense that the SUNY system was a loose collection of what felt like unrelated institutions and making a real, functioning network out of them—one that could best serve New York and New Yorkers. For the last few years we've been calling this transformational phenomenon "systemness"—or finding opportunities where our institutions, guided by the strategic plan, can work together in an optimal way that drives New York's economy and prepares our 463,000 current students, and untold numbers of future students, for the modern workforce and for life.

School districts could take a page out of this plan by encouraging greater collaboration between schools and school leaders.

Coach Bobby Bowden, Former FSU head coach and all-time winningest coach in Division 1 football, discussed how he utilized the servant leadership lens in his five-plus decades of coaching football in the following interview excerpt.

> I view myself as a servant leader. I have always put my players first. I made sure the coaching staff understood that as well. I always felt my job was to help these young men become better men. This means that there were times when I would give them second chances. Sometimes the media and others would criticize me for keeping a player that had gotten into trouble, but I personally felt the easiest thing I could have done is kick them off the team. But I felt like I needed to save my kids and sometimes this meant giving them a second chance. This didn't mean that there weren't consequences to their actions. I would find ways to make them accountable. I might do something like take away housing or make them run extra early in the morning based upon the infraction, but this helped the kids understand that they had to change their ways. Over the

years, there were some who I did have to let go, but my primary concern was for my kids.

This didn't mean that I let players do as they please, or that I didn't take accountability for what happened, because I was the head coach, and at the end of the day, the buck stopped with me, but even my coaches knew that we were there for the players. Some of the players came from broken homes, some of them had no homes or family, so I wanted to give them a chance to make something of themselves. I wanted to make them better players on the field and better men off the field. Even though I coached for over 50 years, I never felt like it was a job, but rather I felt like it was my calling in life.

Imagine if more school leaders felt like their work was a calling instead of a job. They would go the extra mile to ensure that faculty and even students develop their talents and find their passions.

John Baldoni, leadership expert and author of *Lead by Example*, explains how the servant and transformational lenses actually complement each other:

> Servant leadership is all about leading by example. It is predicated on leaders doing what is necessary for the organization to succeed. It means that leaders put people into positions where they can use their talents and skills to succeed. Servant leadership stems from the individual in charge recognizing that he or she can only achieve organizational goals through the collective effort of others. The leader puts him- or herself into a position to serve the organization by setting the right example and holding him- or herself accountable for actions and results.
>
> Servant leadership complements transformational leadership in the sense that if you are going to effect change you must work with and through others. There is a service ethos inherent in getting people to do things differently because it falls to the leader to show the way. He or she does this by setting the expectations, providing resources, providing support and guidance, and evaluating for results. I would imagine this is what successful school leaders do when taking over failing schools.

I think Baldoni makes a great point that administrators can effect the greatest change in a school culture by supporting and empowering their staff to be successful.

Ideas to Try

After you discover your own leadership style, it is important to focus on becoming more of a transformational and servant leader (or developing those styles further if you already exhibit them). While this might seem uncomfortable or even a daunting task, especially if you have worked within the transactional lens, here are some techniques and habits that will help you maximize your leadership potential as you become a more effective leader.

- Encourage and praise *often*. Leadership experts like Abrashoff, Elton, and Baldoni all emphasize the importance of praising your staff loudly and often!
- Focus on developing your staff. Remember the way you treat them will be the way they treat their students.
- Be a source of inspiration, a role model for commitment, perseverance, and risk-taking, with a strong desire to achieve.
- Diagnose, meet, and elevate the needs of other team members by individual consideration, and believe in the improvement of others.
- Be seen as competent, knowledgeable, and deserving of your role in the organization, but also make a conscious effort to be transparent and regarded as all of those things and more, so you can really continue to influence your followers.
- Build community. This is one which is often a topic of discussion, but often has much to be desired in the educational world.
- Value diverse opinions. A servant leader values everyone's contributions and regularly seeks out opinions.
- Help people with life issues (not just work issues).
- Sell instead of tell. A servant leader is the opposite of a dictator. It's a style all about persuading, not commanding.
- Think "you," not "me." There's a selfless quality about a servant leader. Someone who is thinking only "How does this benefit me?" is disqualified.
- Determine what motivates your staff. Motivations change over time and between individuals.
- Think long term. A servant leader is thinking about the next generation, the next leader, the next opportunity. That means a tradeoff between

what's important today versus tomorrow, and making choices to benefit the future.

- Act with humility. The leader doesn't wear a title as a way to show who's in charge, doesn't think he or she's better than everyone else, and acts in a way to care for others. He or she may, in fact, pick up the trash or clean up a table. Setting an example of service, the servant leader understands that it is not about the leader, but about others.

Key Points to Remember: Knowing Your Own Leadership Style

- Transactional style is focused on reward versus punishment and is the least effective style of leadership.
- Transformational style focuses on organizational change and empowering followers.
- Servant leadership style has its main focus on followers.
- Examine leaders you think are effective and identify traits they exhibit. Or read good books on leadership.
- Focus how you treat your faculty or staff, because that is how they will treat students or others.
- Don't let your ego get in the way of effective leadership.

Key 2 | Develop Your Strengths

"Leaders are more successful when they identify and develop their strengths rather than focusing on their weaknesses."

Brad Johnson

As the title of the book suggests, we don't want you to simply be a better leader, but we want to help you maximize your leadership potential. We want you to not only be the best "you" possible, but also lead others in such a way that you help them maximize their potential as well.

The number one reason people fail to maximize their potential is because too much focus is put on areas of weakness or growth rather than focusing on developing strengths. Whether it is a performance review, teacher evaluation, or simply feedback, we tend to focus on areas of growth or weakness rather than on what people do well. This isn't to say that we shouldn't be aware of weaknesses, but if our focus is only on fixing weaknesses, then the best we can hope for is mediocrity. This is a cultural mindset. Just look around and you will see products that advertise to fix our "defects," such as weight loss products or health and beauty products. Do any of these products or ads focus on bettering who you already are or just changing to improve the weaknesses we have?

This mentality also pervades our schools. Students are expected to achieve a minimal score on a standardized test and millions of dollars are spent yearly on improving test scores. What about the student who is struggling in a subject and puts all of his time towards that, while ignoring the subjects that come easy to him? Why is he not becoming even better at those subjects that he already excels in, building his confidence even more, and becoming even stronger in those subject areas? The answer is because the focus is on improving weaknesses and not developing strengths. This leads to an unrealistic belief that only things that are hard or areas in which we struggle must be worthwhile. We have been conditioned to believe the things that come easy to us must not be valuable. But what if that student loved science and could have become a brilliant scientist one day if he got to keep working on it rather than spending all his time on something he struggled with, like history?

Take someone like Michael Jordan, who is considered the greatest basketball player of all time. He recognized a talent and strength in a specific sport and put his focus on developing this strength. In fact, when someone excels in another area of life, they are often equated to Jordan—such as "Tiger Woods is the Michael Jordan of golf." However, did you know that Michael Jordan tried to become a professional baseball player? He wasn't very good and this career path was short-lived. What if he had focused all of his time and effort into becoming a good baseball player rather than focusing on his talents as a basketball player? He would have focused on a weakness instead of developing a strength. We may have missed out on seeing one of the greatest basketball players of all time, because the chance of him being one of the greatest baseball players of all time was probably nonexistent.

People who reach the pinnacle of success in any field do so because they maximize their strengths, not because they focus on correcting weaknesses. In fact, Jack Folkman, co-author of *How to Be Exceptional* (2012), discovered in his research that "what made leaders great was the presence of strengths and not the absence of weaknesses, it fundamentally shifted our view about how leaders can improve. Our efforts to make leaders better had been primarily focused on fixing weaknesses. As we teach people about this research on building strengths, many have an 'ah ha' experience that reinforces their intuition that it's our strengths that make us successful." According to Folkman's research, leaders have weaknesses, but they don't hurt their leadership if their strengths are their focus.

I (Brad) have taught graduate-level leadership courses for a few years and I have found it interesting, actually amazing, that most of my students aren't aware of the leadership strengths they possess. They may have an idea of certain traits they may possess, but never thought of them in terms of leadership strengths. These aren't 20-year-old students still trying to find themselves, but many have been in education for several years and are moving into leadership roles or are already serving in leadership roles. I often receive emails either during the course or after the course from students expressing their gratitude for the role I played in helping them identify and build upon their strengths and talents. Many have said that, even though they may have some sort of leadership role, they never really thought they had leadership traits. Now they feel encouraged and empowered to build upon their leadership strengths and want to help others develop their leadership strengths as well. Many express how much these strengths have also improved their personal lives, too.

Whether you are aware of them or not, everyone possesses talents and strengths. Some are more noticeable, like charisma, dominant size, or even high intellect. However, some of the greatest leaders have been introverts, small in size, or had more EQ (emotional intelligence) than a high IQ. Some people may possess positivity. I think we all can agree that we would rather work for someone who is positive and encouraging rather than someone who makes the Grinch look like Mother Teresa. The key is to determine what talents and strengths you possess, develop them, and maximize them in your personal and professional life. And let's not forget that every expert in any field was once a novice, but they developed their strengths to excel.

What the Experts Say

So why haven't universities, schools, and leadership programs done a better job of maximizing the potential of leaders? One of the reasons some leaders never improve is that they focus more on the people who put them into their position than those they lead. As **Emmanuel Gobillot**, international leadership expert, explains: "in organizations, it is often leaders who chose other leaders. This tends to encourage novice leaders to think of their main constituency as the organization and its leaders rather than their followers." Unfortunately, this causes leaders to focus more on their managers or leaders and maintaining the status quo rather than focusing on the people they lead and becoming a more effective leader.

The second reason is that most leadership programs focus more on administrative type development, such as budgeting, than they do on developing actual leadership skills. **Dr. Gina Ikemoto**, Director of New Leaders, explained some of the hindrances of programs that don't adequately prepare novice leaders. The biggest hindrances: are 1) nonexistent pipeline development strategies, 2) inadequate preparation programs, and 3) district policies and conditions that often hinder instead of enable effective leadership. Organizations that have been successful in growing leadership—especially in the private sector—have pipeline development strategies.

They purposefully identify potential and provide incremental, job-embedded opportunities for those individuals to grow their leadership skills over time. That rarely happens in the field of education.

Dr. Ikemoto was part of the research for a report called *Great Principals at Scale: Creating the District Conditions that Enable All Principals to be Effective*, which outlines the conditions that matter. These include: 1) talent management strategies for teachers—because schools leaders impact student learning primarily through ensuring effective teaching in every classroom; 2) talent management of principals—including not only pipeline development, but also effective evaluation and professional growth for principals such that develop their talents and strengths; and possibly *the* most important condition is 3) authority to hire, manage, and dismiss school-based staff. This means that administrators need to be able to actually lead rather than simply advance the status quo.

This type of authority will also help you surround yourself with people who have different strengths, so your whole team is effective. Lee Iacocca, former CEO of Chrysler, often said that he was smart enough to surround himself with people much more intelligent than himself and then he would get out of their way and let them do their job. What a healthy way to look at leadership. Know your strengths, but check your ego at the door, so you can surround yourself with the best.

Jim Kouzes, expert in leadership development and author of *The New York Times* bestselling book *The Leadership Challenge*, took the time to share his expertise with us on how to develop our strengths as leaders. In our interview, he explained:

> Leadership is an observable pattern of practices and behaviors and a definable set of skills and abilities. And any skill can be learned, strengthened, honed, and enhanced. Certainly some people are better at leading than others—that's true in every discipline—but that doesn't mean that ordinary people can't become extraordinary leaders.
>
> What is required, first of all, is the belief that you can learn to lead. You also need the willingness to become better. No matter how much skill or talent you have, if you're not willing to improve and if you don't believe that you can be better than you are today, then no amount of coaching and no amount of practice is going to make a difference. This may sound obvious, but many subscribe to the myth that leadership is an inborn trait and available to only a few special individuals. Nothing could be further from the truth. We find in our studies, for example, that

the best leaders are the best learners. Exemplary leaders are engaged more frequently in learning activities than those individuals who are rated by their constituents as average or below on The Five Practices of Exemplary Leadership. The more people are engaged in learning, and the more interested they are in learning, the more successful they are in leading.

The leader's primary instrument is the self. That's really all you have to work with. It's not going to be the code written by some brilliant programmer, the smart chip inside the personal digital assistant, or the phrase-turning script of a clever speechwriter that'll make you a better leader. It's what you do with yourself that's going to make the difference. The extent to which leaders become masters of their craft is the extent to which they learn to play themselves. Leadership development is self-development. The quest for becoming a better leader is first an inner quest to discover who you are.

That quest begins by exploring and getting feedback on your current level of skill against some standard of excellence. In our work, we use the *Leadership Practices Inventory*—our 360-degree leadership assessment—to measure current levels of skill, but whatever tool you use make sure it's grounded in evidence and offers a model of best practice.

With the feedback you will gain a set of improvement goals for yourself, and then you can select and participate in designed learning experiences that will facilitate improvement as well as build on strengths. You'll benefit from engaging a coach to help you in determining the experiences you'll need—whether on the job on in the classroom—as well as offer you guidance and feedback along the way. Every world-class athlete has a coach; every world-class leader should have one, too. Also, build a support system. Learning is full of trial and error, making mistakes, and often feeling awkward and unsure. You'll need someone you trust to be there for you when you most need someone to talk to and confide in. It turns out that those who are most likely to improve are those are most willing to ask for help.

While Jim shared his *Leadership Practices Inventory*—360-degree leadership assessment—there are a multitude of tests, such as Myers-Briggs and StrengthsFinders, that can help you identify certain leadership traits or strengths. But there are other ways to identify your strengths. You can probably make a list of talents or abilities that you possess or things that you do well. Remember: there is an array of talents that you may possess. Some of these may not even seem like they are strengths, but when developed they can help you be more successful. Some of these talents include confidence, organization, competition, dependability, the ability to relate, team-building, and risk-taking. When these talents are identified and developed, then they become strengths that help you maximize your potential in both your professional and even personal life. Finally, you can ask your colleagues, or even the people you lead, to share what traits they feel are your strengths. Feedback from others can be very enlightening and reveal talents that you may not have realized you possess.

As we mentioned earlier, understanding your strengths can have a positive impact both personally and professionally. One of our friends and a colleague in the leadership development field, **Sarah Davis**, shared how her strengths helped her in both areas of her life. She shared with us how focusing upon her strengths has not only helped her professionally but has contributed to improving the relationship with her father. Here is her story:

> Growing up, I always had difficulty relating with my father. Even as an adult, there were times when I wondered if he actually liked me. We never seemed to be on the same page—ever. When we talked on the phone, I felt like he was tuning me out within minutes. For example, he would ask me about my day, so I would jump into a story of the unfolding of the day's events. But within a few minutes, he would be changing the subject or try to wrap up the conversation. I became very frustrated and so did he.
>
> Our relationship began to change when he sought my advice and training for his company, when he felt he realized he had difficulty communicating with his employees. I had my father take the Strengths-Finder online assessment and then we discussed his results. His Top 5: Context. Achiever. Activator. Learner. Command. One of the many ah-ha moments was his activator theme, which means action is the only thing that matters to this person. We realized that when we talked he didn't want to hear my stories, but wanted me to get to the point and tell him what I did about it (whatever *it* was). With his Achiever, he was ready to move on to the next subject once he felt his questions fulfilled, even though I may not have felt that way. His high Command made me perceive his quickness to move on as being rude or short. No wonder I finished some of my calls with my father in tears, because we had very different ways of communicating. I'm high Positivity, with a lot of energy

to tell stories and love doing so. I'm also Restorative and love to dig in to issues and talk them through to get to the root of it. My dad was not interested in hearing my long-winded problem-solving stories. After discussing the differences in our strengths, we changed how we talked on the phone. I would think of the top two or three things I wanted to share with him so that he would stay focused and engaged. Understanding his strengths helped him communicate better with his staff, but it also helped bridge a gap in our relationship as well. This reinforced my belief and understanding that developing our strengths not only makes us better in our professional roles, but in our personal lives as well.

This is a powerful point that all leaders should remember. You all have strengths that can not only benefit you professionally, but they can improve your personal life as well, as you focus on what you do well.

Finally, an important point to remember is that you want to maximize your talents, because it is your talents that will make you the best leader you can be. **Sally Helgesen** (ranked 15 in the world's Top 30 leadership gurus) shared with us the time she interviewed a woman who owned several radio stations. Here is what Sally shared with us:

> I remember several years ago interviewing a female CEO who owned several radio stations along the East Coast. I asked her what she felt like was one of her greatest strengths. The lady felt she was best at knowing how and when to fire people. She had a sense of what is in the best interest of employees in her company. When she see them underperforming, she would let them go, but in a way that would help them in the future by helping them focus on what they felt they really wanted to do in life. She actually let me sit in on a conference with one of the radio personalities that she planned to fire later that day. The lady in question was a radio personality but was also a minister in a small local church. In the meeting, the CEO told the young lady that she seemed to be struggling between the two different and demanding vocations and that she really needed to choose one path to really focus on. So, the young lady said she was going to give the ministry a try. Now, fast-forward about 10 years and I was in New York City for a speaking engagement and I just happened to pick up *The New York Times* in my hotel room and there on the front cover was a picture of the woman I saw fired from the radio station, and she had just been named first African-American episcopal pastor. Chills ran up my spine as I thought about

the CEO using her strengths that day to help this young lady find her strengths as well as her true vocation.

As this story suggests, the best leaders know where their strengths are and can articulate them well to their followers. They use them for the benefit of the organization as well as to help their followers succeed.

Ideas to Try

- **Do self-reflection**. This is a great way to determine your strengths. Reflect upon things you do well, or things that seem to come naturally to you, such as public speaking, humor, or a love of learning.
- **Take assessments by others**. Take performance reviews from people you trust and even ask people who work with you, such as people who report to you, and ask them what they see as your strengths.
- **Read leadership books**, translating your "ah-has" into new habits of practice and ways of thinking.
- **Be quick to forget**. When finding yourself dwelling on a mistake, learn from it, commit to what you will do differently, and move on. As they say in sports, be quickly forgetful of past mistakes. One cannot forgive others until one learns to forgive oneself. But remember to be quick to forget when others fail, too.
- **Be willing to make decisions**. Whether you consider yourself an extrovert or an introvert, be willing to think and act on your feet. You have to make decisions, even in a crisis.
- **Use mentoring**. Since we know that many traits can be developed or modeled, connect yourself with a good mentor or mentors. Trusted colleagues are also a great resource.
- **Develop self-awareness**. People have different traits and strengths. Some are planning, some are relational, etc. Be self-aware, so you know what you're good at doing. Develop some areas and accentuate what you do well. For instance, if you are personal, then hire people with more planning and detail. Hire those who help you in areas you may lack.
- **Take an online assessment**. There are many online tests that can help you find your strengths and talents. These can include strengths tests, EQ tests, and many more. While these aren't all-inclusive, they do give you a foundation on which to start developing your leadership talents.

- **Lead with integrity**. A strength that all leaders need to possess is integrity. You will never maximize your strengths if you don't lead with ethics and integrity. Effective leaders are character-driven rather than emotion-driven.
- **Delegate**. Be smart enough to surround yourself with people who have talents that complement your talents. Empower these people to take ownership and watch them rise to the occasion.
- **Be yourself ... with skills**. Emmanuel Gobillot explained in our interview, "Using your personality and everything that makes you in a way that produces results rather than just produces waves. It is a lesson that has taken years to learn. I think ultimately we fear rejection as human beings so much that our need to fit in can sometimes blind us to the possibilities of being ourselves. One day we can learn that the two are not mutually exclusive—I guess you can call that the wisdom that is sometimes brought on by maturity."

Key Points to Remember: Developing Your Strengths

- Focus on your strengths rather than your weaknesses.
- Be self-aware. Knowing what you can and can't do will help you focus on what you can do and what others may be able to do.
- Connect with good mentors or trusted colleagues.
- Lead with ethics and integrity.
- Delegate. You can't do it all alone, so hire people who can help you succeed.
- Reflect: take the time to reflect on what has worked or hasn't worked, and be willing to have this conversation with those you lead.
- Be yourself ... with skills.

Key 3 | Develop Those You Lead

Good leaders lead, but effective leaders empower others to lead.
Brad Johnson

Education has traditionally been resistant to input from the corporate world. Education has often prided itself on being different. While it's true that schools aren't businesses, we discovered through our interviews that effective leadership is effective leadership regardless of whether it is in education, the corporate world, the military, or even in sports. In fact, businesses in many instances have done a better job of moving away from a transactional style of leadership, but education remains deeply stuck in this leadership style of the past. This mindset limits the growth of faculty and staff in most educational settings. For our schools to become world-class and to maximize the talents of our staffs, it is time to focus on empowering our faculties to maximize their potential.

So how do we do that? How do we empower our faculties? How do we help them maximize their potentials? First of all, how well do you even know your employees? Do you know their passions or their goals? Do you know them professionally, or do you also take an interest in their personal lives? Teachers do interest inventories with their students to get to know them. Have you ever done that with your employees? Too often, when a leadership role is taken over from a previous leader, it is assumed that all of the roles in the establishment should retain the status quo, but why? While you need to develop your own leadership skills, you need to recognize that you also need to develop those that you lead.

One of our more dynamic and informative interviews was with Chester Elton, who has been dubbed the Apostle of Appreciation. He was a bundle of energy and insight. One point he made in our interview is:

> Motivators change, so leaders need to be in tune to what motivates people now, not what motivated people three years ago. This is why it's so important to know your people. For example, someone on staff may love the opera, or basketball, so you may reward her with tickets, or additional training, or added responsibility. Find out what people care about and care about them.

However, since education doesn't have the deep pockets of the corporate world, you may find a less expensive but just as thoughtful way, such as a gift card or even supplies.

The mark of effective leaders is their ability to develop and empower their followers. Employees, after all, are the greatest asset an organization possesses and this includes schools. But, as we learned earlier, many leaders work within a transactional (rewards vs. punishment) style of leadership, so the talents of employees are not fully utilized.

Interestingly, Gallup research shows that people who feel like their strengths are utilized in their job are six times more likely to be engaged at work and three times more likely to feel like they have a high quality of life. However, the same research shows that two-thirds of workers *don't* feel like their strengths are being fully utilized. This means they don't feel engaged at work, have lower productivity, and don't feel like they have a high quality of life.

Now imagine if two-thirds or more of employees felt like their strengths were being utilized. Imagine the level of engagement and productivity that would exist. If this were a faculty of teachers, imagine how the students would respond to such an environment. It would impact the entire school community.

Adults aren't different from children when it comes to motivation. If we only focus on areas of weakness, or areas that need improvement, then people will never be intrinsically motivated! However, when you focus on people's talents and strengths, then they can't help but be motivated. In fact, people are nearly 100% actively engaged in their jobs when their administration/leaders focus upon their strengths. When the focus is on improving weaknesses or areas of growth, then the number drops to 78% of people who are actively engaged. Even worse is when administrators ignore their employees, such as with poor management. Then only 60% of employees are actively engaged in their work.

What the Experts Say

In our interview with **Chester Elton**, best-selling author of *The Carrot Principle*, he explained that leaders need to have what is known as an aspirational conversation. Aspirational conversations are ongoing dialogue between the individual and their manager focused on personal development actions to support the expansion of responsibilities, upward mobility, or new career paths. Basically you have to know your staff to know what motivates them and how to make them more effective. In this conversation, there are five key questions to ask your staff on a regular basis, such as during an employee review. So, instead of focusing on areas they need to improve, shift the conversation and ask them these questions:

1. Have we kept our promises to you?
2. What do you think we do really well, such as reading, math, or even extracurricular?
3. What do you see, such as in other schools, that would make us do better?
4. What would make you want to leave us?
5. Where do you see yourself in 3 to 5 years?

People often leave because there is no room to grow. Ask them what their personal vision is. Do they want to be in administration or have they ever even thought about it? Do they want any other leadership roles? Do they want to grow in other ways professionally, like becoming published? Then tell them you will help them get there. For example, let them know that if they will be the best teacher they can be every day for you, then you will help them achieve their goals.

In our interview with Dr. Nancy Zimpher, Chancellor of State University of New York, she explained, "I try to get the right people in the right places. In terms of staff development, I take a page out of Jim Collins's book, *Good to Great*, quite literally. I look to get the right people on the bus, so to speak, and once they're there, I look for the best ways to make the best use of their skills, knowledge, passions, and interests."

Dr. Zimpher further explained:

> Empowering your staff to do the work that means the most to them, that they're best at, leads to building a truly dedicated team, and in the kind of stubborn, complex work we do, that means everything. Different people do their best work in different ways; we have extroverts and introverts among us, people with different strengths and specialties. It's important to trust the people you hire to do the job you hired them to do, give them the room and tools to grow and contribute but also stay close in touch. It's a kind of elastic dynamic that works when you attract and develop the right talent.

Similarly, **Diana Booher**, a Top 21 speaker of the 21st Century, believes that the approach depends on the job assignment of the employee. Leadership is about giving ownership to the employee of their personal productivity and self-improvement. Provide the tools, provide the training, assign work/projects according to strengths, set the minimum standards, set the stretch goals mutually, give feedback and coaching, and provide ongoing resources for their personal access and improvement. The "resources" may include tutorials, a peer mentor, or more training. Effective leaders make sure all these steps and processes are in place—and then demand productivity as part of the "ownership" arrangement.

Jim Kouzes, leadership expert, shared his personal experiences of interacting with corporate leaders on developing strengths of those you lead. Here is an excerpt from our interview:

> When we asked a similar question of Joyce Clifford, former senior vice president of nursing and chief nurse of Beth-Israel-Deaconess Hospital in Boston, she said to us, "I may not be the most knowledgeable person ... but I know how to get other people to think well about themselves." Expressing a similar sentiment, Pete Thigpen, former president of Levi Strauss & Co. USA, and now a fellow at the Aspen Institute, offered this advice: "Really believe in your heart of hearts that your fundamental purpose, the reason for being, is to enlarge the lives of others. Your life will be enlarged also."
>
> Exemplary leaders, like Joyce and Pete, know that they can only make extraordinary things happen when their constituents feel strong, capable, and effective. They know that they must enable others to feel powerful and in control of their own lives. They know that the

motivation to excel has to be internal and that they have to create a climate in which others can perform at their best. When people feel able to determine their own destiny, when they believe they are able to mobilize the resources and support necessary to complete a task, then they will persist in their efforts to achieve.

The only way to create a climate like that is by giving people the chance to use their best judgment in applying their knowledge and skills. That is why exemplary leaders make certain that constituents have the necessary data and information to understand how the organization operates, gets results, and does good work. They invest in people's continuing competence, and they coach people on how to put what they know into practice, stretching and supporting others to do more than they might have imagined possible.

Exemplary leaders also structure jobs so that people have opportunities to use their judgment. They provide others the necessary resources, especially information, to perform effectively. They do away with as many routine assignments as possible, and they find a balance between people's skills and the challenges associated with their work. They continuously educate, educate, and educate. They ask more questions, and give fewer answers. They make sure that people understand the big picture of how the organization operates and how individual jobs help to contribute to that vision. And, perhaps most importantly, they demonstrate their confidence in the capabilities of constituents and colleagues.

There is nothing that can boost the confidence of your staff and make them feel empowered than to allow them opportunities to contribute to the success of your vision.

Dr. Terry Orr, Director of Future School Leaders Academy, shared some insight into how leaders can develop the strengths of future leaders in the educational field. Here are her four suggestions that will give faculty an opportunity to take on added responsibility and see how they handle the role:

1. supporting one teacher in improving his/her teaching based on teacher standards
2. facilitating a small group of teachers or other staff on improving curriculum and instruction to strengthen student learning in a priority area
3. developing a project to engage families or community members that would extend or enhance student learning.
4. do strategic planning around a gap or problem area in student learning.

Key 3

Finally **David Pennington**, president of AASA, shared his experiences in developing others by explaining:

> Administrators need to be looking out for future leaders. Identify people who could be a leader in the district someday. Give people leadership opportunities to grow and develop their leadership skills. Look for things like instructional coaches and curriculum people who may have the potential to be effective principals, for example. Give these individuals opportunities for more staff development and give them more responsibilities. If they have potential, then help them get certifications or what they need to take on new roles.
>
> I also suggest looking for people who work in extracurricular activities. This is because they learn how to lead. Some people tend to think there are too many coaches in leadership, but think of the leadership experience many of them possess. They have to deal with parents, students, and pressure to win, and much more. Coaches who have coached for a while have had parents in their office angry about something and they had to learn how to deal with them. So, these people have had experience making tough decisions and having hard conversations that leaders typically experience. These people have demonstrated they can respond to a crisis and not be overwhelmed.
>
> I think it's important to look for teachers who are willing to step up and help in other roles, such as committees, board-level committees, or other extracurricular activities. Leaders need to encourage people to take on new roles as well. Some teachers may have never thought about becoming a leader or even see themselves in that role. So, it's important to encourage them and then give them opportunities to develop. You have to look within to find the diamonds in the rough.

Effective leaders will seek out those with potential even if they don't see it within themselves.

Ideas to Try

- **Leave the "buts" behind**. How often have you seen, or experienced yourself, a quick observation where the administrator tells you "Good job" and, instead of leaving it with the "good job," just seems to have to add a "but …"? We recommend, leave the "but" behind! Sometimes you simply need to give praise and leave, or simply get your butt out of there!

- **Find out what motivates your staff. Arthur Carmazzi**, the world's Top 10 leadership expert, reinforced this concept during our interview when he explained, "One of the best ways for a leader to get buy in is to find out the motivators and what is important to the people who you will lead (not relating to increases in salary or less work)." This may mean doing an interest inventory, conducting interviews, or taking the time to just sit and down and get to know your staff and what motivates them.

- **Strengthen your constituents' competence and confidence**. Try the following simple exercise. Before every interaction—whether it's a one-minute, one-on-one conversation or a one-hour group meeting—ask yourself this question: "What can I do in this interaction so that this person (or persons) feel(s) more powerful, confident, capable, and self-determined than before this interaction started?" If you do that, and then act on your answers, you'll be continuously developing and motivating others.

- **Delegate leadership opportunities**. Give faculty members an opportunity to showcase their leadership potential. This is not simply giving them busy work. Let them chair committees, become department/grade-level chairs, or take ownership of a project. Trust that the people you lead can become leaders as well.

- **Allow people opportunities to fail**. Give your faculty the opportunity to try new things and if they fail, that's OK. Failure is a very important part of learning and growing. Provide a safe environment where they can take risks and know it is OK to fail.

- **Treat your staff like adults**. Some leaders treat their faculty like they do students. But this creates a divide between the staff and leadership. You shouldn't need to babysit your staff. Treat them like adults. Remember: the way you treat your faculty will be how they treat their students. Give your faculty reasons and opportunity to stretch out on their own and even lead others.

- **Appreciate their efforts**. Yes, it's true that people get paid for the job. But we know that teachers don't work just for the money. Empowered people need a greater level of satisfaction than simply financial stability. They need to feel that leadership appreciates their contribution and values their participation.

- **Share leadership vision.** Help people feel that they are part of something bigger than themselves and their individual job. Do this by making sure they know, and have access to, the organization's overall mission, vision, and strategic plans.
- **Communicate effectively.** Make certain that you have given people, or made sure that they have access to, all of the information they need to make thoughtful decisions. One of the biggest ways to demotivate people is to have expectations that haven't been effectively communicated.

Key Points to Remember: Developing Those You Lead

- Focus on empowering your staff.
- Provide praise often and publicly.
- Provide opportunities for faculty to lead and give them some power with the opportunity.
- Provide them with a safety net to fail.
- Communicate effectively.
- Treat staff like adults.

Be a Leader, Not Just a Manager

Effective leaders know how to manage things and lead people.
Brad Johnson

The educational leadership role is one of the most demanding positions in any field. Leaders are often brought into districts, schools, or even departments to "fix" problems such as test scores, low graduation rates, or other issues. This puts a lot of pressure on leaders to make changes quickly. Unfortunately, this tends to place all the focus on short-term solutions without giving much thought to long-term consequences or long-term solutions to best guide a school. There are many tasks that must be attended to daily which are administrative in nature; however, leading the district, school, or department should always be the main focus.

Many people assume that being in a position of management also means that person is a leader. But are they synonymous? Should they be? Can they be? Do people who manage also effectively lead? Here are some characteristics and traits of managers and leaders from leadership expert Warren Bennis in his book *On Becoming Leaders*:

- The manager administers; the leader innovates.
- The manager is a copy; the leader is an original.
- The manager maintains; the leader develops.
- The manager focuses on systems and structure; the leader focuses on people.
- The manager relies on control; the leader inspires trust.

- The manager accepts reality; the leader investigates it.
- The manager has a short-range view; the leader has a long-range perspective.
- The manager asks how and when; the leader asks what and why.
- The manager has his or her eye always on the bottom line; the leader has his or her eye on the horizon.
- The manager imitates; the leader originates.
- The manager accepts the status quo; the leader challenges it.
- The manager is the classic good soldier; the leader is his or her own person.
- The manager does things right; the leader does the right thing.

As you can see there are actually some needs and benefit from both styles. For example, it is important to have short-term goals. However, if your vision is only on the short term, it can lead to long-term disaster. We call this walking off the cliff, when you are so focused on something in front of you that you don't see the big picture. This is also the difference between a transactional leader, who is focused on the moment, versus the transformational leader, who is focused on change and improvement that is long term and sustainable. Long-term solutions and success are the mark of an effective leader.

Major corporations, universities, businesses, and countless individuals have examined the traits to compare the aspects of managing and leading. There is a distinct difference between managing and leading. When looking at the list of comparisons above, it is easy to conclude that managers live in the now and leaders look to the future. A person who manages is focusing on completing a task or a job, but after that is completed there is no looking ahead to what is next.

Basically it is like managers are checking off lists with no overall plan or goal. A leader does not work with that stagnant mentality. Leaders will also get tasks done, but with an overall goal in mind. A leader works along with the team instead of dictating to the team members. Leaders are the ones fostering and generating new ideas that will carry us into the future.

So, effective leaders are forward-thinking. They look at problems, not just for their immediate attention, but for long-term effect. How many times have you seen a district adopt a new program because it was popular or other districts saw improvement, without giving thought to the long-term effectiveness or need of the program? Then, within a year or two, they adopt a different program and begin again.

Leading is a paradigm shift from managing. The assembly-line model that promotes managing is becoming archaic. Leading supports collaboration, which is the way our business and lives are changing to. Just think of how we communicate now in the working world. Skyping, videoconferences, and webinars are just a few ways that we communicate. No longer are people flying across the ocean for a meeting; instead, they are opening their browsers and talking via computers. Numerous software programs are available for collaborative projects. Forbes recently shared and rated collaboration tools such as the Gnatt Chart, the Kanaban Chart, Basebcamp, and Asana (http://www.forbes.com/sites/allbusiness/2013/07/11/5-types-of-office-collaboration-tools-which-is-right-for-your-team/) to show which are best for collaboration in the workplace. No longer is there one manager overseeing workers beneath them. There are collaborative teams with leaders among them.

It is apparent that the paradigm shift from manager to leader is being recognized within our colleges, too, because new degrees are being offered, such as Organizational Leadership, Outdoor Leadership, and Worship Leadership, just to name a few. While Business is still one of the most sought-after degrees, the programs include courses on leadership skills and collaboration, along with the traditional accounting and human resource courses.

Although several preparation programs are attempting to partner with districts to provide internship opportunities, they continue to be too focused on the nuts and bolts of leadership such as budgeting, human resources, and other administrative type duties, rather than developing leadership skills.

What the Experts Say

Dr. Gina Ikemoto, Director of New Leaders, explained in our interview:

> Our programs are aligned with the 70-20-10 research on leadership development, which suggests that 70% of the development should be focused on practice, 20% on coaching and communities of practice, and 10% on formal knowledge. Too often, traditional preparation programs spend 70% on the formal knowledge piece. This means they don't spend enough time developing the important leadership talents of the individual.

What this means is that our preparation programs are still spending too much time on formal knowledge of becoming an administrator rather than on developing future leaders.

So where does that leave administrators within our schools? Do they manage or do they lead? What about department chairs, principals, teacher-coaches, learning specialists, or anyone in the position of authority who leads a group of people or students? Do these people have the tools it takes to lead instead of manage?

Forbes listed the eight characteristics of effective school leaders. They include: having consistent, high expectations; constantly demonstrating that disadvantage need not be a barrier to achievement; focusing on improving teaching and learning through the use of professional development; expert assessment of pupil development; developing individual students through rich opportunities inside and outside of the classroom; cultivating partnerships with parents, business, and communities; and self-evaluation with goals for improvement (http://www.forbes.com/sites/nickmorrison/2013/12/30/the-eight-characteristics-of-effective-school-leaders/). These characteristics all show the school leader is constantly looking towards the future. The idea of managing needs to be a thing of the past and our administrators within our schools need to be leaders.

As **Judy Vredenburgh**, Director of Girls Inc., explained in our interview, "An administrator needs to possess both management and leadership traits, but that career advancement usually requires evidence of leadership accomplishment and not simply efficient operational administration. Bringing strategic, results, and change orientations, which are important components of leadership to an organization, is integral for effective organizational performance." This means that, while administrative skills shouldn't be discounted, it is more important to possess true leadership traits for optimal performance within an organization.

But perhaps Emmanuel Gobillot, international leadership expert, offered the best advice on understanding the importance of leadership over management in his interview response, stating: "The key to success for a novice leader is to understand that leadership is both not about them and at the same time all about them. It is not about them, as the focus should be on what followers need to be effective, and all about them, because by being the best and most skillful version of themselves they can be in a position to answer those needs."

He shared more insight into the administrator/manager vs. leader, as he believes that a person needs to possess skills of both to be most effective in a given role. He explained,

> Most of the time I admit to finding the discussion leader vs. manager tiresome insofar as I believe you cannot have one without the other.

In fact, in recent years we have put so much emphasis on leadership that we have lost a sense of good management practices. In many of my interactions with newly appointed leaders I find them unable to set goals and manage performance in a way that good managers would do and that used to be trained in organizations. My take is that leadership and management go hand in hand, which is why I shy away from the distinction and encourage anyone to think about the needs of their followers. I find that more productive to the practice of great leadership.

Ideas to Try

We have provided several ideas that will help you transform into a more effective leader rather than just a manager. While it might be overwhelming to implement all of the ideas, you can choose two or three that you feel will be most beneficial first, and then over time you can implement more of them.

- **Focus on the big picture**. It is easy to get caught up in the day-to-day operations of a school. However, if you focus only on short-term solutions the big picture needs of the school population can be missed. If you focus only on the day-to-day operations, you may resolve an issue one way, but it may be detrimental to the bigger picture or long-term success. Leadership is focused more on solutions that are effective in the long term.
- **Analyze yourself:** Use the list of items above from Warren Bennis, and do a serious analysis of your own beliefs and behaviors. Where do you see yourself in each comparison? Can you justify why you would be one way or another? What can you conclude about your own leadership qualities and styles? Do you feel you can be an effective leader? Being honest with yourself is necessary and crucial to being a leader.
- **Take a survey**. There are numerous surveys that you can take to analyze your own leadership skills. By searching on the Internet, you will be able to find already made surveys as well as software and companies that will custom-make surveys to fit your specific needs. After you analyze your own skills, use the surveys with anyone in a leadership position. The surveys will help you learn about skills that your employees

and co-workers have that can build a stronger team and promote more leadership opportunities.

- **Focus on your strengths**. Whether it is from survey results or from just knowing what you are good at, focus on your strengths. Often people tend to focus on weaknesses, but they need to do the opposite. Goals can be made to improve weaknesses, but strengths need to be cultivated and allowed to continue to grow. StrengthsFinder is an online assessment which I (Brad) have used with my graduate students to determine their top leadership strengths.
- **Do scenarios and role-playing**. Role-playing and acting out scenarios is an effective way to model and handle situations. The role-playing should include unrealistic and realistic situations that can occur within the workplace. It should also include role reversal where faculty and administration play in each other's roles. This change of perspective often opens up new ways of seeing events that can occur.
- **Ask, "What are *our* needs?"** By analyzing the needs at your school, you will be able to set up a program that will allow leadership opportunities and collaboration to occur. The analysis should include input from different members. This will help faculty and staff to feel valued, and also help with buy-in for collaboration opportunities.
- **Consider leadership training**. Be willing to attend or send people to training opportunities dealing with leadership skills. This will help to bring in the newest techniques available. It will also help people feel like they are valued and part of a team that will lead others.
- **Focus on transformational leadership**. Transformational leaders inspire, empower, and consistently praise their staff. Transactional leaders tend to work within a reward vs. punishment mindset. Staff is treated more like students than adults and it creates an "us vs. them" mentality. A transformational leader is focused more on staff than on self.
- **Be seen, heard, and be there**. Leadership guru John Baldoni shared with us that there are three essentials for becoming an effective leader. Be visible in the hallways and classrooms, rather than locked up in your office. Not only should your vision and goals be heard, but also take the time to hear what is going on within your school, among your staff and students. Finally, be there for whatever your staff needs. As the quote at the beginning of the chapter suggests, carry the water for your staff, so they can focus on getting their job done.

Key Points to Remember: Being a Leader, Not Just a Manager

- Recognize the differences between being a manager and a leader.
- Know your own strengths as a leader and build on those strengths.
- Design a plan for your school to fit your specific needs.
- Be willing to send faculty and administrators to professional leadership training.
- Think long term (see the big picture); forward-thinking.
- Develop a more transformational leadership style.
- Be seen and be there for your staff.
- Attend workshops, professional development, and even read good books on leadership.

Key 5 | Find Your Voice

"Finding your voice begins with positive self-talk."
Brad Johnson

Once you realize the importance of leading and not just managing, you can develop your own voice. *Voice* is creating an overall expression of who you are … to yourself, your community, and to the world. This voice will allow you to communicate your needs and wants while contributing your talents and capabilities. Your expression is the culmination of finding, creating and using your *voice* to make a difference for yourself and your life. Discovering your values, creating outcomes, sharing your influence, developing courage, and conveying your overall expression are all ingredients for finding and using your *voice* as a leader. In our schools, there are numerous opportunities to become leaders. Besides the typical administration roles, teachers can have leadership roles such as grade-level chairs, department chairs, and instructional coaches. The guidance counselors and support staff also have leadership roles. All of these positions will not only have different roles and responsibilities, but will also have different personalities, which means they all need to find their own voice that will not only help each individual succeed, but enable them to successfully work together, too.

As we have learned throughout the book, focusing on your strengths and developing the strengths of those you lead will make you and your staff more successful. So, part of finding your voice has already been accomplished by understanding your talents and strengths. For example, some people may not feel like they are a leader or possess the skills to lead, so they never find their voice as a leader. However, understanding that you possess talents and strengths and have been placed in a leadership role because of certain competencies should help you realize that you do possess the potential to be an effective leader.

Part of finding your voice begins with believing you actually can be an effective leader. This is what we refer to as self-talk, where you think you can be successful. Do you have self-doubt of belief in your ability to be successful? Successful people focus on the things they do, not on what they need to improve, and this empowers them with confidence to lead. It in essence gives them their voice. Finding your voice will give you competence as a leader, boldness to make tough decisions, and confidence to be yourself rather than just another administrator who simply wants to fall in line and never question anything.

What the Experts Say

One key to finding your voice is explained by **Rachael Robertson**, leadership expert and Antarctica Expedition Leader, who shared in our interview:

> A leader needs to know, with absolute clarity, their purpose. That is, why they do what they do. There will be many great times and there will be many tough times, but if you understand why you chose to be a leader it will keep you resilient. Many people forget that leadership is a choice. Knowing why you chose to be a leader in the first place keeps you focused. For example, my purpose for my team in Antarctica was "to make every single person feel like they were making a valuable contribution to the expedition, and for the rest of the team to know that contribution."

So, in other words, having clarity of purpose is critical to "your voice."

Unfortunately, novice leaders tend to focus simply on maintaining status quo. This means they often acquire or mimic the previous voice that was once in that position. This can be because they are afraid to rock the boat and make changes too quickly. It could also be because that is what they saw modeled and they imitate what they know. Teachers are well-known for doing that same thing. Teachers often teach the way they were taught when they were in school. We model what we know. We know what we experience. When someone moves up in a position, it is normal to model what was previously experienced. This is more like managing than leading.

However, to be a truly effective leader and maximize their potential, they will have to find their own leadership voice. **John Chubb**, Executive Director of NAIS, explained in our interview,

> Principals in public schools are not rewarded for being leaders, but are rewarded for following rules and that is why they are managers instead of leaders. By giving the principals and anyone in a leadership role the tools to find their own voice, they can move beyond the managerial role and into a true leadership position. There is a real difference between leadership and management. When people first get into a leadership role they don't really understand it. There are tasks to be done and it's now their job to get those tasks done. This can be a department chair, lead teacher, principal, or even central office personnel. People often move into a job where the skill set is connected to their past success, but they don't have a lot of leadership experience. You may understand technical tasks, but not leading others. This is true in business as well as education.
>
> Training is much more focused on nuts and bolts, like school law, governance, budgeting … you know the technical aspects. But, what's missing is the focus on what it means to be a leader. Like inspire people with a vision. Most people don't think leaders have any vision. So set goals, get everyone working together. Use your people skills.

Christina Parker, Executive Director of GAYC, reinforced the view that we have to move beyond the managerial role mentality to find our leadership voice. As Christina explained in our interview:

> I think, first and foremost, people need to recognize the difference between a manager (typically promoted based on competencies in areas of expertise and the ability to check things off a list) and a true leader before they can start to find their voice and start to figure out their style. For me, it took a lot of self-reflection and figuring out what helped to move the team forward versus what just simply got the tasks done. You know that you are entering the true leadership area when people are no longer following you because they have to (positional), but because they want to as a result of what you have done for the organization as well as what you have done for them. Something that really helped me define my leadership style was asking questions and listening to other leaders as well as reading many books. As I would read the books, I would write notes in them as

to how it related to the current leadership situation that I was in, and then I would always list three things I learned and three action items that I would personally work on. I would then come back and follow up in a couple of months to see if the three things that I had learned had come into focus more now that I had practical application, and I would also check in to see that I had completed the three action items. I am continually putting conscious effort into growing my leadership style. I think that true leaders are lifelong learners and never satisfied with the status quo.

Dianna Booher, a top leadership expert, explained the importance of finding your voice as moving from a transactional style of leadership to more of a transformational style of leadership, She explained:

> A novice leader typically leads by authority of a title or position. But that same leader must quickly grow so that he or she can lead by personal authority—a much broader and deeper well of influence. The quickest route to personal influence as a leader is to model the actions and decisions of respected, experienced leaders. As you approach various quandaries, situations, decisions, think, "How would this experienced person handle this situation?"

Leaders show their ability to lead by demonstrating these key characteristics:

- concern for those they lead
- an attitude of continual learning and willingness to seek guidance
- confidence that allows risk-taking
- integrity.

With these attributes on display, people recognize the seeds of greatness developing in a leader—if those leadership skills haven't indeed flowered to full bloom and maturity.

Ideas to Try

How to find your voice—answer the following questions to help find your own voice:

- What do you **value**? Knowing what you value tells a lot about your own character. Virtues such as ambition, respect, honesty, patience, compassion, thankfulness, empathy, curiosity, creativity, and flexibility are essential when being a leader. Being able to recognize and model your own values will help you when finding your voice. Those values should be the undertone to your voice. Once you identify what you value most, then be sure to recognize when others model those values.

- What are your **passions**? Ideally, if you find your true passion, then you will be happy for life. Being in a position or at a job that you are not passionate about will limit your potential and stifle your creativity. Those who are supposed to follow your lead will know that you are not passionate about your career, and that can negatively impact everyone involved. Finding your passions can be a challenge, but it is worth the time and effort. Research, brainstorm, and even be willing to try new things. Once you find your passion and are able to transfer those passions to your career, then you will find a voice that others will want to follow.

- Who would you **imitate**? While some say imitation is the finest form of flattery, others say that it more important to be yourself. But think of why you would really imitate someone. What qualities do they have that you admire? Those are the qualities that you need to recognize and find within yourself, if possible. Just think of being able to have a list of people who you admire and taking the best qualities from each person.

- What type of **personality** do you have? Are you an extrovert or an introvert? Are you a type A? Are you confident? Are you emotional? Are you proactive or reactive? How do you react in a crisis or a challenging situation? There are numerous personality traits, and knowing your personality will help you to be able to find your own voice. It is important to be aware of how you will react in situations. This will help you to be better prepared when those situations occur. Your voice represents your personality. When you can recognize the qualities that you possess, then you are able to start to recognize the personalities of those you are leading.

- Can you **articulate a thought or idea**? Finding your voice and communicating your thoughts have to go hand in hand. Can you speak in front of a crowd or audience? Can you articulate your thoughts when put under pressure? Can you get your voice across in writing as well as verbally? Are you comfortable communicating in any means necessary, whether it is face-to-face, conference call, Skyping, FaceTiming or any

- What are your **strengths and weaknesses**? While this may sound like a cliché type of question, it is important. You should focus on your strengths and develop those as much as possible. Too often we focus on weaknesses and do not enhance the strengths we already have. Your voice should represent the strengths that you possess. You can always try to work on weaknesses if the need arises, but enhance the strengths and make sure they resonate in your voice.

What is your **managerial style** or **philosophy**? Knowing your managerial style will help you to have a consistent voice. Do you believe in a servant style or do you have a transactional or transformational style? Is there another model that fits you better? Once you recognize your managerial style, then your voice should represent that style. This will be a constant that the people working with you can count on.

What to do once you have found your voice:

- **Creating your outcomes**. Finding your **voice** means **creating your outcomes** to get what you want and need. Start by establishing your goals. Recruit a team that will help to reach the goals. Then build a roadmap, whether on a dirt path or a concrete highway, so the resulting journey is one worth taking. Charting your map, articulating the plan, and sharing the vision shows you can handle the smooth or bumpy roads with lots of detours along the way.
- **Influence others**. Finding your voice means learning how to **influence others**. Once you have identified your values and outcomes, how do you influence yourself, your environment, and those around you, to maximize your opportunities and results? It is essential to use good communication skills when trying to influence others. These communication skills include being clear and concise as well as being able to listen effectively. Always keeping in mind your values as well as the end goal will help to successfully influence others.
- **Take risks**. When you find your voice, you must be willing to **take risks**. Taking risks means that you are willing to experience failure. This speaks volumes to those who are working with and for you. Lessons are learned through experiencing failure. By you having an active

voice in the process and being one who also takes risks shows you are a team player and that you care about the process and the people.

- **Communicate effectively**. When using your voice, be sure to communicate effectively. Choose wisely the tools for communication and be thoughtful and articulate when using your voice. Miscommunication can be traumatic and cause unwanted and unnecessary situations to occur.

- **Develop the courage**. Finding your **voice** means developing the **courage** to do what you know is right, no matter how scary it may be. Courage comes in many shapes and forms and can be needed at the most inopportune time. It could be finding the courage to speak up in a meeting where you may be the youngest or the lowest-ranking member of the group. It could be finding the courage to trust others in a plan you have developed when you know you will be held responsible for the results. Do you have the courage to change direction even if the new direction is not the most popular? What about having the courage to stand alone in a crowd?

- **Remember those virtues**. When you use your voice, be sure to keep virtues in mind. Be respectful in every situation. Leaders often have uncomfortable situations or circumstances that occur. Being respectful when using your voice can make the best of any situation. Being sarcastic, demeaning, or disrespectful, while tempting at times, should never occur when expressing your voice. Take the high road and remember your voice represents what you value.

- **Brainstorm! Brainstorm! Brainstorm**! Make lists and keep adding to them. This can be for anything listed about in regards to finding out about what you value, what you feel are your strengths and weaknesses, who you would imitate, and so on. I am a list-maker. I like to keep a list of traits that I value not only in myself but also in others.

- **Take a personality quiz**. There are numerous personality quizzes available. Taking one may seem beneath you or goofy, but it is worth it. I have actually taken dozens just to see the results. I like to analyze data and see what traits appear to be recognized continuously among these quizzes. At first I was surprised that what I thought was my personality was totally different than what the quiz results showed. Then, as I read the descriptions and took more quizzes, I finally got an accurate picture of my personality.

- **StrengthsFinder 2.0**. Reading this book and taking the online assessment is something recommended to me by a friend who was taking over her nursing division at a local hospital. She had used it for herself and then with her own children. I highly recommend reading this and taking the assessment. Your strengths may surprise you! It is a lens that I was not used to looking through, but have been glad that I did!

- **Make a plan**. This includes a plan for learning about you, as well as planning outcomes. Design a plan on how you will best succeed when finding your voice. Once you have found your voice, plan for the outcomes you want to see happen. Remember: change is hard, but often needed. Make sure to have a detailed plan designed before you share it. Then, be willing to listen to others and give them a voice in the application of your plan. **Practice public speaking**: Finding confidence speaking in front of others is a talent. Practice speaking in front of a mirror. Enroll in a public-speaking course. Finding your voice is a challenge, but having your voice heard is an art. This is one of the most important aspects of voice. Making sure your voice is heard will allow results to happen. It is almost a waste to find your voice and then never be heard.

- **Fail and model courage**. Don't hide when something you have done fails. Model to others that failure is a vital part of growth and learning. Once you fail, voice that failure and then voice how you have the courage to continue, and formulate a new plan. Hiding failure will not help with growth. Having the courage to voice failure, even though it may be the hardest thing you have to do, is what leaders have to learn to do.

- **Put yourself in uncomfortable situations**. You have to be put in challenging situations in order to grow. Find courage to speak up and insert your ideas. I remember the first department chair meeting I sat in. I made it a goal to ask one question, just to see what it felt like to talk in that setting. I often volunteer to speak in front of groups just to challenge myself and overcome that possible fear I may have.

- **Leaders show their ability to lead by demonstrating these key characteristics**:

    - concern for those they lead
    - an attitude of continual learning and willingness to seek guidance
    - confidence that allows risk-taking
    - integrity.

- **Read about leaders you admire**. Read leadership books from people you admire and make notes of traits they exhibit or ideas they share, and then incorporate them into your leadership style.
- **Self-talk**. What is the tape recording that you play over and over in your mind? Do you have positive thoughts and feed on your strengths? Or do you have negative thoughts and question your abilities? Successful people feed on positive self-talk!

Key Points to Remember: Finding Your Voice

- Know your purpose. Your voice represents you and is an expression of who you are.
- Your voice can change in reaction to different situations and responsibilities. But, even though it changes, there should be some underlying characteristics that do not change—for example, your values/integrity.
- Remember that everyone has a voice. Listen and recognize others' voices and what they are trying to share.
- Speak up and be heard, but be respectful and virtuous in the process.
- A novice leader typically leads by authority of a title or position. But that same leader must quickly grow so that he or she can lead by personal authority—a much broader and deeper well of influence.
- As a leader, be mindful to give back to your community.
- Make your self-talk positive!

Key 6 | Influence School Culture

"Schools are influenced more by their culture than by policies and rules, but leadership influences that culture."

Brad Johnson

When we think of how a school functions, we think of the policies and procedures that have been set in place. However, as the quote suggests, policies and rules do not necessarily define the functioning of a school or school system. However, the culture—which refers to the beliefs, perceptions, relationships, attitudes, and written and unwritten rules that shape and influence the school—often defines the school or school system.

If you have spent any time in the educational world, you realize that rules do not always define the workplace. But, good or bad, culture often seems to define the nature of a school or even school system. Take, for instance, the Atlanta Public Schools where there has been an alleged widespread cheating scandal. Twenty-one teachers and principals have taken plea deals and 13 more will actually go to trial. Some of the plea deals included fines and restitution of up to $50,000.00, as well as up to five years of probation and up to 1,000 hours of community service. Unfortunately, this type of scandal is not isolated to the Atlantic Public Schools, but further investigations found that there have been hundreds of school districts around the country with highly questionable swings in test scores and more investigations into a widespread "culture of cheating."

A toxic environment was created in this specific instance where policies and rules were largely ignored and improved tests scores at any cost became the culture of the school district. Otherwise, how can one explain how in such a noble profession that teachers, principals, and even system

Key 6

level leaders disregarded the very rules and policies that they helped create and that they expected their students to follow? This shows the powerful influence of culture on an organization.

The fact that culture has such a strong influence on schools or any organization is not necessarily a bad thing, but it is up to leadership to ensure that it is a positive and effective culture. In many instances where there are issues, it can often be traced back to a negative or toxic cultural environment. And you don't need scandals or widespread arrests for a negative school culture to exist.

Unfortunately, many people who are in administrative positions are equipped to handle the "academics" of a school, such as testing and data collection, but have very little experience or expertise in influencing school culture. As we have mentioned, administrators are often placed in their roles because they have performed well in previous positions, so they have more expertise in the academics of school rather than in the relational or cultural nuances of a school. But groups such as the National Institute of School Leadership believe principals need more training—not just on data and academics, but also on how to build relationships and support for learning among staff and students.

What the Experts Say

Research suggests that school leaders who attend to their school culture see improvements in areas from teacher satisfaction to student achievement. As Dr. Terry Orr, the director of the Future School Leader Academy at Bank Street College of Education in New York City, explains: "There is more research on best practices for evaluating and improving school climate," but "the emphasis on a positive, developmentally appropriate learning culture for students has gotten a lot less attention in recent years with the focus on accountability."

Poor leadership can create a negative culture that may affect school performance more than previously thought. One research study found that leaders who have been trained to understand how relationships and values interact in a school can improve their campus cultures, and that those without such a conceptual understanding still have an "accidental influence" on their campuses, but it is not always a healthy one. This means that schools may underperform simply because the leadership is not in tune with the culture of the school.

So, what does this negative school culture look like and how does it exist? If you have administrators who have been successful in previous roles, and not necessarily patient with other people, they think they need to just go in and do everything themselves. The worse the climate, then the less they use interpersonal tactics to engage a variety of people, when in fact this is what they need to do. As Dr. Orr explains, "a new administrator is usually under pressure to fix a problem, such as test scores or school morale, so they feel like they have work in an almost transactional style of rewards versus punishment. However, a novice principal can't transaction her way into a positive school culture."

In a negative school culture, teacher relations are often conflictual: the staff doesn't believe in the ability of the students to succeed, and has a generally negative attitude. A negative culture will even affect attitudes toward spending time to improve instruction and motivation to attend workshops. According to Dr. Orr, there are several major factors associated with a negative school culture, which include:

- work in an autocratic (transactional) style because of pressure to make changes quickly
- lack of a clear sense of purpose or direction
- ineffective response to crisis
- vision or values don't align with what they are actually doing
- ineffective use of resources.

While there can be many factors that attribute to a negative school culture, many of them are associated with the major factors. For example, if a school says it values all students and wants resources used equitably, but it limits advance placement (AP) courses or limits special education opportunities, then resources aren't being used equitably and conflicts with the school goals. Or, if an administrator wants to build trust with the staff, yet never engages them positively, develops their strengths, or utilizes their abilities, then there is a disconnect between the vision and what is actually being done.

When a negative culture is created, it affects the functioning of the whole school. In a negative culture there is poor communication among staff, students are often blamed for lack of progress, collaboration among staff is discouraged, and hostility among staff can be commonplace. This culture creates an environment where teachers may be disengaged and students become discouraged, disconnected, or simply endure the school day.

Key 6

Now that we have an idea of what a negative school culture looks like, we will now examine the factors that will create a positive culture. The most important aspect of a positive school culture is effective leadership. As the last part of the quote above suggests, leadership will actually define the culture of a school. Therefore, it is important for the leadership to set the tone of the school rather than let the culture of the school dictate how leadership reacts. Leadership is a thermostat for the school, not a thermometer. So how can effective leadership create a positive school culture? According to Dr. Orr, here are a few factors to focus upon in creating a positive school culture.:

- have sense of vision and purpose
- have clear values and let them direct policy
- create student-centered mindset
- use of resources should reflect values
- response to crises should be effective.

As you can see, these factors are greatly influenced by the leadership of the school. In fact, these can be influenced without a lot of outside input from the district level, which means a school's success in reality does rest on the shoulders of the principal and leadership team. A negative culture doesn't mean that the school has failed, but rather that poor leadership has failed. However, effective schools are always reflective of effective leadership. So, make building a positive school culture the priority from day one.

Renowned leadership expert Chester Elton also weighed in on developing a positive culture when we interviewed him. He said, "When someone takes on a leadership role, 50% of people will buy in because you have the title, you will have to prove yourself to 25%, and 25% may never buy in because you're not their leader. So the new leader has to focus on either changing that 25% or helping them move on to another job or career." This is why it's important for leaders in education to have more authority when it comes to hiring and firing, and shows the importance of having an effective leader to create a positive culture. Elton also said, "To create a positive culture, you have to talk about the culture that you want in the school, such as great teaching, more extracurricular, etc. We are what we talk about. People forget numbers and data but they remember stories." Finally, he shared, for a great culture to survive in a school or any organization you need to live by the "Rule of Three":

1. Be world-class (Whatever your focus, make it the best).
2. No surprises (if something is wrong, I want to hear from you not from someone else).
3. We are here for each other (We don't backbite or fight).

In my graduate classes, I (Brad) have students read books on leadership from a variety of leaders in different fields. These are students who will soon be taking on leadership roles in their schools, and I like to expose them to a variety of different leaders and leadership styles. One of the books I have them read is *It's Your Ship*, which is about the experiences of Captain Mike Abrashoff aboard the USS *Benfold*. Because so many students have been influenced by his book and leadership, I was fortunate enough to interview Captain Mike Abrashoff for this book. His leadership style and story is one of the best examples of how culture influences a school or any organization. The story is basically how he took the worst ship in the Navy and transformed it into the best ship in the fleet by changing the culture of the ship.

In 1997, the USS *Benfold* had a change in leadership and a new captain, Mike Abrashoff, was to take over as commander of the ship. His first experience was the reception aboard the ship to bid the former captain farewell. The crew seemed glad and relieved that the former captain was leaving. It turns out that the former captain was a very intelligent man, but made the crew feel inferior and was condescending to them, which negatively affected the culture of the ship. The ship's performance was ranked last in the fleet and the crew didn't feel safe should they be called into action.

Abrashoff recalled, "As I watched the ceremony that day and the reaction of the crew, I wondered to myself how the crew would react when I leave the ship after my tenure as captain?" He said this put things into perspective quickly for him. He knew his goal was to focus on improving the morale of the crew. He said, "At this point in my career, other than sinking the ship, I knew I was set as far as retirement and even advancing in rank, so my goal wasn't to use the appointment to simply advance. Instead, I wanted to make a real difference in the crew of this ship."

Over the course of his tenure as captain, Abrashoff implemented many strategies which helped build a positive culture. For instance, he created an environment where crew felt safe to take risks and take ownership in the crew's success. As Abrashoff replied, "I took responsibility for the actions of the crew, so they knew I had their back, even if they failed." Captain Abrashoff would also publicly praise the crew when they did good work—in fact, the crew affectionately named him "Mega Mike" because he would constantly praise his crew, which improved morale.

Sounding as much like a college coach as a ship captain, he said the reason that he felt like he needed to focus on the crew was that he wanted the parents of these young soldiers to be proud that their children were under his leadership. So, he didn't see them just as a crew, but he got to know them personally and found out their interests and their strengths, so he could best utilize their talents aboard the ship. Over the course of approximately two years, Abrashoff so profoundly changed the culture of the USS *Benfold* that it went from being the worst ship in the Navy to the best ship in the fleet.

Interestingly, as his time as captain came to an end, he decided that he didn't want the traditional pomp and circumstance given to such an auspicious occasion, but rather he had 310 lobsters flown in for the last dinner with his crew. As he said, "I knew many of them had never seen, much less eaten, a lobster." Then, the next morning, rather than the traditional ceremony, which he had experienced when coming on board, he simply gathered his crew around him on deck in their working coveralls, and gave what is the shortest change of command speech in military history. He simply told them, "You know how I feel." He said he left that day with pride, not so much for making the ship the best in the Navy, although that was great, but that he left an accomplished, tight-knit, effective crew that he was unabashedly proud to have commanded.

After the interview with Abrashoff, I realized that as a leader he did influence the culture of the ship, just as the captain before him had influenced the culture of the ship, as well. Under the leadership of one captain, the ship and crew were seen as the worst in the Navy, and yet, with different leadership and a positive change in culture, the same crew became the best ship in the fleet. I can think of no better example of just how important culture plays in the functioning of an organization, and how important leadership is in influencing the culture.

Ideas to Try

As you can see, the story of the USS *Benfold* reveals similar circumstances to that of a school. Principals are like the captain of the ship, who often have to work with whatever crew is already on board. As you have seen from the experts who have shared their expertise throughout the book, the principles of effective leadership are consistent regardless of the organization or field.

Therefore, we have provided some of the most important strategies that can be incorporated by a school leader to improve the culture of any school. While it might be overwhelming to implement all of the following ideas, you can choose two or three that you feel will be most beneficial, and then, over time, you can implement more of them.

- **Create a clear vision and sense of purpose**. Have a clear vision for your organization will help cultivate a positive environment. Articulate that vision effectively, so the staff is on board with you.
- **Have clear values and let them direct policy**. Make sure your core values are reflected in your decision-making. This includes the use of resources to reflect your values as well. If they do not align, then issues will arise.
- **Become a "Mega Mike."** Celebrate successes in staff meetings and ceremonies. Tell stories of accomplishment and collaboration whenever there's an opportunity.
- **Create a student-centered mindset**. Remember that you are there for your students. They are the customer and should be at the forefront of every decision in some capacity.
- **Create a safe environment to fail**. Take responsibility for your staff. Give them the opportunity to take risks, be creative and innovative, and assume ownership without fear of punishment, even if they fail.
- **Don't neglect the school culture**. This may seem odd or a given for this section, but allowing the culture of the school to develop by default is a sure way to produce a toxic culture. What are the perceptions, relationships, and attitudes of your staff?
- **Use proper communication**. Make sure communication is clear and that it reaches everyone intended. Sometimes communication doesn't reach its intended audience and this can cause many unintended issues. Ensure communication flows vertically (top to bottom, and bottom to top, as well as horizontally.
- **Consider community connections**! Many parents who weren't good students still shy away from school. Reach out to them. Make everyone feel like part of the team! Include the community, or even bring the community into the schools with partnerships.
- **Follow the Rule of Three**. Be world-class; No surprises!; and We are here for each other.

Key Points to Remember: Influencing School Culture

- Have a clear vision of direction for school.
- Empower your staff to take on responsibilities and take risks in a safe environment
- Be seen, heard, and be there for your staff and students.
- Promote "we" among the whole staff.
- Celebrate successes of everyone!
- Focus on developing strengths and talents of your staff.
- Good leaders lead, but great leaders empower others to lead.
- Remember the Rule of Three.

Be Accountable to Those You Lead

"The best leaders understand they are also accountable to those they lead."
Brad Johnson

No word invokes more emotion in education than the term "accountability." With initiatives like *No Child Left Behind* and *Race to the Top*, accountability continues to be a focus in education. The debate for more intense accountability is met with pros and cons. The problem with accountability in education is that we have developed a culture where no one is expected to fail. On the other extreme, metrics have been put into place for the sake of accountability that are misguided or can be inaccurate and misleading.

Accepting Responsibility

At its essence, accountability is about "walking the walk." It is about using the pronoun "I" when you need to be accountable for a decision or an action. Accountability is the guiding principle that defines how we make commitments to one another, how we measure and report our progress, how we interact when things go wrong, and how much ownership we take to get things done. It is, in essence, the nerve center that runs throughout every part of the organization and through every working relationship, to every member of every team.

A great example is how a good coach reacts to a loss. When you hear a coach like Nick Saban at Alabama speak after a loss, he rarely blames his players for the loss, but rather he explains that he is accountable because he didn't prepare his team properly. Similarly, Coach Bobby Bowden shared the same sentiment during our interview when he said he was just as accountable to his players as they were to him. He explained that, while they were there to play football for him, he was there to help his players be better men on and off the field, and that he took that responsibility very seriously. While there is no "I" in team, these coaches reflected the accountability of their leadership with the pronoun "I."

Understanding What Went Wrong

Accountability is important when things don't go according to plan. As a leader, you are responsible and should acknowledge that to those above and below you. However, acknowledging this is not the same as understanding what went wrong. Being accountable does not mean simply accepting responsibility and ignoring true cause-and-effect relationships. If things go wrong, you should look into your organization to understand what happened. The organization should have the same feelings of accountability. The time to build these feelings of accountability is before something goes wrong, not during the investigation.

In order for you to know what went wrong, you have to make it a priority to rehash the situation. Was the fault truly yours? If so, own it. Let others see or know that you made a mistake. Modeling failure can be a powerful tool. Some of the best lessons learned are through failure. But don't just stop there. Make changes if necessary to make sure the mistake doesn't happen again. Figure out what the problem was, and then modify and adjust.

There are times when leaders take responsibility or are held accountable because "the buck stops here," so to speak. They are responsible for those under them, so ultimately they need to be held accountable. So, in this type of situation, recognize the responsibility and be accountable, and then go back to your team or those involved in the mishap, and figure out what went wrong. Together solve the problem. Do not play the blame game; take the high road. Those involved in the situation will know whose work caused the problem and they will also then know who worked together to solve the problems. It is important that the person knows you took responsibility, but do not make it a punishment. Instead, make it a learning experience. The wrongdoing needs to be noted, so it does not happen again and people do not think that is acceptable. But belittling people will do nothing for morale.

Taking the Good with the Bad

Accepting responsibility does not always equate with the bad decisions. Often there are many excellent choices and decisions made that you should also be held accountable for. Do not sweep those under the rug. Do not ignore them. You should celebrate those and make those public, just as you would admit to wrongdoing. Take credit when credit is due. There is a balance between celebrating and bragging, so be careful. But it is important for those who you lead to see you recognize your own excellent work as well as theirs. Being proud of accomplishments and successes shows you are passionate about your job and those around you. Realistically there was probably a team who helped you, so celebrate with the team. This will also make it easier when a mistake occurs, since you will be able to experience success and failure together.

Creating a Culture of Accountability

By you modeling accountability, others will follow. Too often accountability equates with fear. People fear to fail. They fear for the ramifications if they do something wrong. They fear the unknown, because they often do not know who will be held accountable for what action. First of all, communicate that you as a leader are ultimately responsible. Own and model that role. Next, make sure those working with and for you know you want to create a culture that promotes accountability in a positive light. By creating a culture of accountability, people will be more likely to accept responsibility and be willing to grow from situations dealing with being held accountable. Here are a few suggestions on how to create a culture of accountability:

- *Set clear expectations.* This means for yourself and for those who work with and for you. Think of it almost like a rubric for a teacher. If you know what you have to do and the requirements expected, then you will more likely successfully complete the task. This is the same for those working under you. How can you be held accountable for something if it is not clear what needs to happen? This is the same of your employees. How can you expect to hold them accountable if they are unclear about the goal?
- *Know the consequences.* When people know the consequences that can occur if something goes wrong, it often gives a clearer picture of the expectations and why something needs to occur.

Key 7

- *Model failure and show growth.* By modeling your own failure, others will know that failing is normal. The key to failure is showing growth from the failure. By displaying both the failure and the growth, people will begin to trust in the fact that, not only will they fail, but also that failure is expected at times and the growth is what is celebrated.
- *Reflect.* Reflecting includes both celebrating success and making plans for future changes. There are times when people need to be held accountable for successful decisions and goals. Celebrate this accordingly. There are times when failures occur, and being held accountable means owning them and making new goals to continue.

What the Experts Say

David Pennington, President of AASA, explains,

> Part of accountability is being willing to change your mind. If you make a mistake, then just admit it and correct it. For example, if you make a decision about the conduct of a student, such as suspension, but find out that the information you received was wrong or new information is revealed, then be accountable for and change your decision.

This is an important lesson, especially for novice leaders, who may be feeling like they can never be wrong or don't want to be seen as a weak leader. The truth is, people respect honesty, and when you are accountable for your actions, even wrong actions, people respect it and will be more willing to follow you.

As leadership guru John Baldoni shared in a personal interview,

> a leader has to be there for whatever is necessary or the urgency of the moment." You have to be accessible for your staff, not hiding in your office. As he explained, the leader has not only to lead by example, but do whatever the team needs to succeed. Leaders believe in holding themselves accountable/responsible for the cause. Leaders encourage team members to hold the leader accountable, and when leaders are held accountable by the organization they are able to hold others accountable for supporting the team in meeting campus expectations and goals.

Being accountable and holding others accountable is twofold in transformational leadership. Take responsibility for your actions.

Another aspect of leadership that deals with accountability is authenticity. Authenticity for a person in authority is what contributes to a leader's presence. Presence is what I call "the right stuff of leadership." It is an expression of character focused on doing what is right for others and the organization. Fundamental to authenticity is accountability. The best way to destroy authenticity is to fail to hold yourself accountable for results. A leader who shares credit when things go right, and stands first in line when things go bad, is a leader others want to follow. They regard that person as authentic.

It's important to build a culture where people want to be accountable and would rather do anything than let you down and then results will take care of themselves. People think accountability is punitive or getting in trouble. And leaders think it is like holding a gun to their head. But, in reality, accountability is about relationship. A leader is accountable to helping followers be successful. A leader is accountable to their staff. It's not just about the staff being accountable to the leader. The leader is accountable to them; they don't owe the leader anything. The leader needs followers more than followers need this specific leader. Finally, a leader will help go the extra mile for a teacher. A leader could help a teacher get an advanced degree to help them move into a leadership role. For example, the leader might teach a class for them if they need to leave early for class.

Sam Silverstein shares that there are no excuses for a leader. Some people think having a good excuse is acceptable, but it's really not. He shared that his barber was often late to open up his shop for his appointment. One morning, the barber was late because he got a speeding ticket. The barber felt like this was a good excuse for being late, and he knew if he showed the barber empathy and accepted his reason for being late that his behavior wouldn't change. Instead, he asked him why he got the ticket. Was it because he was running late? When the barber confessed that he got the ticket because he running late again, they discussed that he needed to be accountable for his actions, that if he left in time each morning that he wouldn't be late. This is a great point about accountability, because often we see people who have poor habits, such as arriving late to school, leaving early, or some other habit that needs to be corrected.

Key 7

There are no excuses, they simply need to be accountable for their actions and change them, even if it requires leadership helping them make those changes.

Dr. Gina Ikemoto, Executive Director of New Leaders, reflected on the importance of accountability by explaining:

> Leaders should be held accountable to schools goals, which—for public schools—are about preparing students to be successful in college, careers and citizenship. These goals should be shared goals with their followers, including staff, parents, and community. In order to effectively lead, you need to get people to follow you. In order to get people to follow you, you need to do many things. You have to be inspirational. You have to be an effective communicator. You have to be reflective and open to feedback. This often means being accessible and inviting feedback from followers. Using 360-degree feedback—from teachers, parents, students and supervisors—can be an important source of data about leadership practice that should be triangulated with other sources of data to assess leader performance and hold them accountable. This type of data helps us to know whether leaders are being effective in implementing the leadership practices that we know will help them achieve student outcome goals.

As the Chancellor of University of Illinois at Urbana-Champaign, **Dr. Phyllis Wise** had some great insight into leading with accountability. In our interview, she shared her views on accountability:

> I think accessibility and accountability are key components in differentiating leaders in practice from leaders in name. In my opinion, you need to be every bit as accountable and accessible to your team as they are to you. A big part of effective leadership is based in mutual trust—and this can't develop if the people working for and around you don't see you working as hard as they are and holding yourself up to their expectations. And this is closely tied to accessibility. As chancellor—I have enormous authority over my own schedule. I can close my door or limit my interactions with staff, faculty and students. And while in some respects that might make a day easier for me, it would actually take me out of the organization and create a huge disconnection between me and the university community that I am

charged with serving. I can't be a good and effective leader if I'm not immersed in this community and if my door, literally and figuratively, isn't always open.

Individuals who end up in leadership positions are often the most ambitious, but leadership takes far different skills than those used for personal gain. Once leadership is attained, your worth becomes far less about what you personally accomplish and much more about the success of the team, or in my case the success of the university. That means fostering success for others and finding satisfaction in the accomplishments of others, not just getting co-authorship or invitations to sit on boards or adding more lines to adorn your resume. Leadership is in many respects a service role. And it takes a great deal of humility to listen, consult and solicit criticism from others.

A great point she makes is that you really have to set your ego aside to be a truly effective leader.

Finally, **Marty Zimmerman**, 360 leadership guru and retired Marine, really grasped the concept of accountability as he explained in our interview:

While leadership is earned, there are varying levels of authority which attend leadership. It could be hire/fire authority, the authority to spend money up to a limit, or even the authority to sign contracts binding to the organization. This authority goes beyond just responsibility. Responsibility could be typing a letter for the boss to sign. Besides typing it, signing it could illustrate the authority part of it.

As a leader, I believe carrying out the authority we have feeds into our accountability to exercise that authority properly, and to not abuse that authority, or "power." This often gets into the political discussion and tension between, say, the White House and Congress.

When thinking about authority, the word "delegating" comes to mind, as well. Delegating is not about just responsibility by itself (which is assigning a task, not delegating). Delegating includes responsibility accompanied by handing over some authority, with limits. This could include authority for someone to communicate directly with the CEO of the organization's major client to maybe spend so much money without seeking approval.

So, when leaders talk about surrounding themselves with good people, inherently the "good" includes people who recognize accountability and practice it themselves. "Good" people go beyond simply being "talented" or "gifted" people. It suggests people who follow through, which is a natural consequence of accountability.

I think Marty reinforces that accountability in leadership doesn't just flow from the bottom up, but, more importantly, a leader, such as a principal, is just as accountable (if not more so) to his or her staff.

Ideas to Try

- **Be transparent**. Transparency is in essence of accountability. When people see the how and the why of your decision-making, then they are more likely to accept your decisions. Leaders who work in the shadows are in fact "shady" leaders.
- **Give and take**. This means to give more credit to others when things go right and to take more of the blame when things go wrong. If you want a staff to follow you to the ends of the earth, so to speak, give them more praise and accept more of the responsibility yourself. Great coaches are known to do this, and it's a great trait to possess in any leadership role.
- **Delegate**. This means, when you give someone a goal or task, then also empower them to make decisions in the process. An individual held accountable to meeting a goal (or goals) should be fully empowered to make all decisions. This cannot be top-down decision-making. Let people be accountable and make decisions to drive the final goals of the corporation.
- **Giving account**. That is simply the narratives (i.e., stories) we make up to explain what is going on—we give accounts. Giving an account is different than responsibilities. Responsibility is about explaining why something happened (backward-looking), and giving an account of what is happening or going to happen is forward-looking.
- **Communicate clearly your expectations for yourself—to everyone**. By informing your people about what you are doing, and what you expect of them, one can create a better culture of trust through accountability.
- **Consider employee engagement**. Staff will be more willing to put in the necessary effort when they know their leader(s) are "open book" and willing to accept feedback.

- **Follow up**. Don't give out tasks without some kind of follow-up or follow-through. For those of you who believe you are good at follow-up, look around your office, home, and garage, and see how many unfinished projects stare back at you. If nothing stares back, you can say you're good at follow-up.
- **Lead with integrity**. The best way to be accountable is to do things the right way. When people know their leader is ethical and leads with integrity, then they will be more willing to be accountable for their actions as well.
- **Lead by example**. Let your staff see that you are willing to do anything you ask of them. Be willing to jump in and get "dirty" when needed. Be a "do as I do" leader, not a "do as I say" one.

Key Points to Remember: Being Accountable to Those You Lead

- Be forward-thinking.
- Give praise and accept responsibility when things don't go right.
- Be willing to admit your mistakes (this one is huge!).
- Lead with integrity.
- Be transparent.
- Follow up with projects, committees, programs.
- Delegate (with some authority).
- Be willing to jump in and get dirty when needed.

Key 8 | Communicate Effectively

"Communication breakdowns occur whenever there is more than one person in a room."

John Baldoni

As a leader you are responsible for effective communication, but do you know all that entails? When you communicate with others, do you think of body language and facial expressions? Do you have a hard time choosing how to communicate, whether it be face-to-face or by using technology? Are you aware of cultural barriers? Do you listen as well as you talk? Do you talk too much? How is your grammar? Can you take criticism and do you welcome communication back to you? Do you know how people of this generation communicate? Are you aware of the harm that can be done if miscommunication occurs? These are just a few of the questions that you need to be considering every time you communicate with someone. Communication is not a simple concept; it is complex and can be vital to your success as a leader. Let's take a look at some of those concepts in more detail.

Miscommunication is the Root to Most Problems

Miscommunication is a major reason for misunderstandings or things quickly going wrong. Clarity is key. A single instance of miscommunication can undo numerous hours of proper communication. People tend to remember the negative and forget the positive. That is also true for miscommunication; people will hold on to that instance longer than when things are communicated properly. Wrongly telling information can cause huge setbacks in work and in morale. *As a leader you are not only responsible for what you say, but also for what others understand.* This is where miscommunication usually occurs. It is delivered in a way that you think is fine, but due to lack of clarity or some other aspect it is not received how you meant it. Being specific, to the point, and not saying too much will help alleviate this problem. Being too wordy or giving too much information can cause miscommunication. How the message is delivered can also cause miscommunication. Hearing something versus reading something generates two different responses. Not going to the source and talking directly to people can also be a cause of miscommunication. For example, address specific issues with the individuals in question, do not generalize—otherwise, you leave everyone disenfranchised. You have got to make sure that others understand what you are trying to communicate. This takes practice, patience, and the willingness to correct the mistake when it is made.

Michelle Boyea, Vice President of McKesson Pharmaceuticals, explained the importance of effective communication in our interview. She said:

> The best way to communicate effectively is to keep it simple. In fact, if I am sending out important information to a large group of people, especially if it is something I have been involved in creating, I ask someone to read over it who isn't as attached to it, and see if it makes sense to them. If not, then we discuss it until it makes sense and we rewrite it. The mistake is assuming that everyone understands a topic to the extent that you do, when that simply may not be the case. It is important for everyone to have a common set of knowledge on a given topic to move it forward. This helps everyone understand goals, expectations, and ensure everyone is on the same page.

Generational Differences: Texting, Email, Tweets, and Technology

Here are some staggering facts that we need to keep in mind: Facebook has more than a billion users worldwide; in 2012 there were over 200,000 texts sent every second (just think of what it is now); there are over one million users on Pintrist daily; the average number of tweets every day is 58 million. Communication now occurs daily on a global level.

How do you communicate? Are you even aware of these different ways of communicating? Do you send group emails and hit "Reply all" to every response? Do you direct message? Do you Skype or videoconference? Do you expect your workers to reply to communications within a specific amount of time? Do you respond to their communication with you in a specific amount of time? Do you have company policies on how and when social media can be used in regards to communication? Have you provided your workers with training on how to successfully and even more importantly, safely use social media? As a leader, you have to be "in the know" and be able to communicate in any way that people communicate with you. Sometimes this means choosing the correct format. You are not going to tweet something that should be said in a face-to-face conversation. You can save your business thousands of dollars in travel expenses if you can Skype, FaceTime, or videoconference. Unless, of course, it means more to actually be there face-to-face with the people with whom you want to communicate. These are all choices that you need to make. Communication is about building relationships and engaging with one another. Do not let generational differences get in the way.

Does Grammar Matter?!

A fellow English teacher often wears a shirt saying, "Let's eat grandma. Let's eat, grandma," showing how commas save lives. While humorous, it is often not funny when grammatical mistakes are made when communicating. We need to keep in mind that language and grammar rules evolve and different forms of communication have their own languages. Yahoo recently had a story on how the most popular word for 2014, "emoticon," was not even a word at all. So now talking with symbols and abbreviations is not only acceptable but also overwhelmingly popular. As a leader you need to know when grammar matters—for example, if you are writing a formal letter or issuing a contract grammar matters. Anything in writing represents you, so what do you want it to say?

Do We Listen to Understand or Listen to Reply?

We have two ears to listen and one mouth to speak, so shouldn't we take a hint from that? According to research, we listen at a rate of 125–250 words per minute, but think at a rate of 1,000–3,000 words per minute. Listening is one of the hardest things to do, often because we don't take the time or we are emotionally invested in what we are saying. We are often quick to reply without taking the time to first understand what has been said. There are actually listening skills that can be practiced to help make you a better listener. Being a good listener will help build relationship skills and increase your effectiveness in your job. Knowing how important listening is, can you believe that research says we remember only about 25–50% of what we actually hear. If this is the case, how can we assure that the important part of what is being said is actually being remembered? Not listening can be directly correlated to miscommunication. Tools such as active listening, repeating to make sure you understand and clarify what has been said, can help enhance listening skills. Taking time to digest and make mental notes can also help improve listening skills. As a leader you should be listening to understand and then be prepared to reply.

Take the High Road!

Too often we talk about each other instead of talking to each other. We want to join in on putting someone down or talking bad about a job that has been done. While it may be hard to confront someone about a situation or tell them exactly what you think about a job that has been done, that is your role as a leader. You need to take the high road and be honest. This can be done respectfully and professionally. Keep the person's feelings in mind and treat them how you would want to be treated. Modeling this will bring respect and trust. Talking about people behind their backs or spreading rumors is unprofessional and should not occur. Effective leaders work to create an environment among the entire organization that encourages dialogue among peers in an effort to improve work production. Creating this type of environment will promote a healthy and dynamic workplace.

Do You Communicate Too Much?

Overcommunicating can lead to being ignored. The first time I saw a colleague use "TLDR" ("too long, didn't read"), I laughed out loud! It was the perfect response, and now I use it whenever it applies. It usually only takes one instance of responding with that to let the sender know they are sharing too much at one time and that I cannot possibly comprehend it all. We are busy people who function in a hectic world. Taking time to read long emails is not the purpose of sending an email. According to the Radicati group, a technology market research firm, by 2017 there will be over 132 billion emails sent daily in business alone. This does not include personal emails. Think before you send an email. People who get hundreds in their inbox are not going to read them all—they don't have the time! And, please, only hit "Reply all" or get involved in group chats in rare circumstances!

Do You Have One-Way Conversations?

Administrators that tend to "tell" rather than have "dialogue" are not effective leaders. It is fine to tell someone what you think or what needs to happen, but always give them the chance to respond. Yelling and walking away shows a lack of respect and often demeans the person. This goes back to the type of managerial style to want to convey. While it is hard to maintain virtuous behavior, remember that your actions and words represent who you are. Take time to plan out what you are going to say and then be willing to have a conversation and not a confrontation. Communication is a two-way street; effective leaders are comfortable with communication flowing back up to them and know how to deal with it once it's received. Do not be reactive. Being reactive often leads to being regretful.

Are There Cultural Differences?

This topic is more important than ever, because we live in a borderless world. We communicate internationally on a daily basis. Vocabulary, dialects, and nonverbal cues are just a few of the major differences that can occur with communication. There are cognitive and emotional constraints that can limit or challenge effective communication. For example, in some countries it is disrespectful to look someone in the eye when talking, while in others it is respectful. In some countries, business leaders tackle numerous agenda items at one time, while in other countries they take items one at a time and will not go onto the next one until the previous one is resolved. No matter the challenges, maintaining personal relationships and making an effort to understand different cultures can help enhance communication and hopefully lessen the amount of miscommunication.

Key 8

Do You Pay Attention to Nonverbal Communication?

Communication is not just about what is said, it is also about how it is said. This includes facial expressions, eye contact, gestures, posture, and body language. According to research, 55% of a person's meaning is in the facial expression, while 38% is in tone of voice and only 7% is in the actual words. With these statistics, I would say nonverbal communication is a skill that leaders must master. Being aware of your own nonverbal skills is where leaders should start. Recognize how you are standing, what gestures you are using. Nodding along when others talk or slamming a fist on a desk can give off two distinctly different messages without ever saying a word. Folding your arms in front of you gives off the impression that you are closed to hearing what is being said. Tone of voice and how you accent your words can mean just as much, if not more, than the actual words. People react with feelings, so by using feeling with your words, the communication can be more effective. Leaders must be able to control their own body language, facial expressions, and hand gestures, but also be able to read others. Recognizing the nonverbal cues others are giving off can allow for more effective and productive communication.

What the Experts Say

Arthur Carmazzi, international leadership and communication expert, believes that leadership communication requires awareness of our own reality and knowing how it affects our expressions, perceptions, listening, and speaking so we can transcend the barriers of this subjective reality. When we do, the emotions that hinder its effective interpretation can connect with and give meaning to others at various levels of inspiration, action, clarity, and emotion. Carmazzi notes that when leaders accept that common sense is filtered through perception, and is not "common" at all, this causes misunderstanding or miscommunication. Realizing this can help them deal with the situations intelligently so they can achieve the intended objective. Carmazzi is a proponent of the **Colored Brain Communication model** (www.coloredbrain.com), which focuses on the ability to manage personal expectations when communicating with people who process information differently. The Colored Brain model helps to understand why and how communication breaks down and helps you learn how to solve it.

Dan Domenech, Executive Director of AASS, addressed the problem with lack of communication. He states,

> some people see information as power and try to keep it to themselves. But that is a mistake. Information is power to the extent that you use it and share it with others to accomplish your goals. Some people are afraid of sharing information, especially bad information, so they hold on to it. However, when the bad news is exposed, and it usually will be, then major problems occur.

By not being transparent and upfront you end up paying the price. Being upfront and transparent is critical to being a good leader.

Dianna Booher, a Top 100 Thought Leaders on Leadership and communications expert, shared with us the five most important traits in regards to communication:

- **Authenticity**: What leaders say must match who they are and what they do. When others discover a discrepancy between words and character, or between words and actions, they will always disregard the words and believe what the actions demonstrate. Once followers lose respect for the leader's character, influence disappears quickly.
- **Honesty/directness**: Leaders must be truth-tellers—even when the truth is painful and even when the news is negative. Nothing restores respect and builds credibility for leaders more than when they have the courage to tell the bad news as directly as the good news: "I don't know," "This project will be risky," "Our team did not do well," or "I failed you this time."
- **Clarity:** Leaders need to master the fundamental communication skills: writing, presenting, public speaking, leading a productive meeting, giving feedback, inspiring a team, engaging others in their vision. Common to all these communication skills are mastery of the language, emotional maturity, and a deep understanding of human psychology.
- **Approachability:** Leaders need to demonstrate humility, friendliness, and vulnerability.
- **Concern:** Leaders who show genuine concern for those they lead win the confidence and commitment of their followers.

Boohler shares the most common issues with miscommunication:

- **Vague word choices**. For example, a leader says we can't bid on that project because we have "limited resources" this quarter. (Equipment? Workers? Raw supplies? Supplier-partners to help? Upfront cash to fund the project?)
- **Missing details**. What a leader assumes is obvious is not always obvious to the listener.
- **Disorganization** (in written documents and in presentations). Communicators provide required details of a situation or an issue—but they are out of place and listeners or readers fail to grasp their relationship or significance to the situation at hand.
- **Facts presented as reasons**. That is, people present facts, data, or other information but fail to interpret that information in light of the decision or issue. Facts are never reasons—unless they are interpreted to tell a story and support a point of view.

Dianna's points on communication should remind us all that miscommunication can cause many unintended consequences. Being clear, concise, reflective, and honest is key to effective communication.

Ideas to Try

- **Be aware of your own nonverbal traits and skills**. Make it a point to recognize your own traits in regards to nonverbal skills. Some people even keep a journal of traits that they tend to use regularly. Makes notes about how you react in different situations. Then, when a situation arises, you can coach yourself to make sure your nonverbal cues are appropriate. This does take practice. Remember: you want to be proactive and not reactive. Your nonverbal cues can give away your reactions before your words ever do.
- **Practice listening**. Tell your coworkers you are practicing improving your listening skills. This alone will make them feel valued. Listen to what they say and then repeat a summary of it back to them, to clarify that you are not only hearing but also processing what they are saying. The more you practice this, the better listener you will become.

- **Remove distractions**. When you are in a position where communicating is important, be sure to remove any distractions. Turn off cell phone, put other work away, and go to a quiet area. This is not the time to multitask!
- **Record yourself**. Video or tape yourself giving a speech or presentation. This will give you extensive feedback about your communication skills. You can do this as a trial or actually do it while you are giving your speech. Consider it like game films! Athletes do this all the time to improve. Why shouldn't you?
- **Read books and articles on communication**. This is a wonderful way to learn about new ways and more research about communication skills.
- **Find courage**. Stepping outside your comfort zone and finding courage to communicate in certain situations can be rewarding. After trying to communicate in an uncomfortable situation, be sure to **reflect** back on the experience and learn from it.
- **Find your voice**. Be sure to know what your voice is before communicating. The only way to communicate effectively is to know who you are and what you represent. Chapter 5 ("Find Your Voice") can help you with this!
- **Have a clear vision for the future and develop a predictable, public strategic plan**. It is critical to have a clear long-term vision for an organization and to have an equally clear and public strategic planning framework to guide decisions at every level. This is how you can empower every individual to make choices and take actions that are consistent and that are always moving you forward.
- **Solicit a diverse set of opinions to ensure the best set of solutions**. Diversity is not merely bound to race, but extends to culture, religion, geography, sexuality, age, gender, beliefs, values, and experience. Historically, diversity has been linked primarily to considerations of fairness, but we have moved beyond that—and beyond just numbers or quotas. We have a record, unfortunately, of leaving some of our best and brightest minds out of our conversations in this nation—and that assertion extends into the higher educational arena as well. That must change quickly and permanently. The challenges our society faces are too complex, with consequences for failure too high, for us to face them without every talent at our disposal. The more perspectives you can bring to focus on an issue, the better your chances are of arriving at thoughtful and successful solutions.

- **Communicate goals clearly and frequently.** It's important to be able to speak well as a leader. But this does not always mean it is necessary to use poetic language or inspirational phrases. Sometimes those tools are useful to inspire an audience, but the most important thing is not to lose the central message. A clear and direct style is simple and effective. The people who work with and for you shouldn't have to guess about your priorities and your vision for the institution.

Key Points to Remember: Communicating Effectively

- Miscommunication is the root to most problems and can be avoided if you use proper communication skills.
- Nonverbal cues matter more than verbal statements.
- Practice communicating. It is a talent that needs to be nurtured.
- Understand with whom you are trying to communicate.
- Finding your own voice is a must before you can communicate effectively.
- Less is more when communicating: too much communication can bog people down and they can lose interest.
- Engage a diverse set of opinions. Respect must be at the forefront of all communication.
- Don't be afraid of generational differences! Jump right in and learn the current communication tools. You want to be leading the way!

Key 9 | Lead with Wisdom

"True wisdom is built on a foundation of ethics and integrity."
Brad Johnson

When you hear the word wisdom, what image does it elicit? For many, we think of an elder man or woman who seems to have figured out the meaning of life. It is interesting that this image of wisdom deals with a concept beyond just applying knowledge, but it provokes a deeper meaning with an ethical or integrity foundation to it, which we will examine in this section as well.

When educators are placed into leadership roles, there seems to be an expectation that they are fully prepared for the role. There is tremendous pressure to be effective, after all you are the one who was chosen for the position. This pressure can be isolating, because novice leaders may not want anyone to know they don't have all the answers. While you may not have extensive experience in your present leadership role, you do have experiences that can help you make wise decisions in your new leadership role. This "wisdom" in the traditional sense usually means having experience, knowledge, and good judgment.

While these are important characteristics, wisdom of effective leaders also includes a value or integrity component as mentioned above. I (Brad) have taught graduate-level courses in leadership for the past several years. One of the courses I teach is "Ethics in Leadership." In this course, I emphasize the importance of wisdom built on a foundation of ethics and integrity. This is a theme among many leadership experts. Steven Covey, for example, emphasized a moral compass in leadership where not just any values were important, but that a moral conscience should be the foundation of effective leadership. As we mentioned in the culture section, there are instances even in education where leaders wander off the path of wisdom and integrity and wind up in a lot of trouble. However, there is no place in education for a lack of integrity or wisdom because we are dealing with our most important resources: our children.

In our interview with Christina Parker, Director of GAYC, she explains the integrity part of leading wisely as

> Integrity has to be the most important part of it. Your words and your actions have to match up in and out of your work environment. People are observing you all the time and honestly, they are formulating their opinion of you the most when they see how you react when times are hard and it is more difficult to act with integrity then when times are easy.

Bruce Lloyd, leading with wisdom and international leadership expert, reinforces this idea as he explains:

> wisdom is not so much about technical bits of information, such as application of knowledge. But it is about relationships with others. Wisdom has a value component to it. When you lead with values then you are leading with wisdom. Knowledge is about the use of information (data) but wisdom tells you how to put this information to good use. Wisdom is the vehicle we use for integrating our values into our decision-making processes. It is one thing to turn information into knowledge that makes things happen, but it is quite another thing to make the "right" things happen. How we actually use knowledge depends on our values. Just because you use something or do something, doesn't mean it is a good thing or good use. Many leaders use information but there are some who don't apply it in a good way.

Leadership is, after all, in part about making good decisions. But decisions can have wide-ranging implications, so it's not just about the moment. Remember: good leaders are forward-thinking, not just reactionary, so how does a decision affect others and how does it affect others long term? These are all part of leading with wisdom.

Novice leaders lack experience in their roles. Wisdom is one trait which novice leaders are expected to utilize, but with a lack of experience this can be a daunting task. But there are traits that new leaders can develop to help them lead wisely. First of all, a leader has to be competent. This is often true of administrators who can organize, plan, and have basic knowledge.

A leader also needs to be confident. If you don't believe in yourself, no one will. But don't be overconfident, because the reality is that people want to know what you know for sure—and what you don't. A confident leader has the ability to be persuasive. However, a leader doesn't have to be perfect; leaders do make mistakes. But when you build trust, relationships, and valued-centered foundation, people will believe in you and your credibility. Image is everything, and the belief people have in you, your mission, and your reputation are key to being a great leader.

David Black, in his book *The Leadership Mandate*, explains some of the characteristics of leading with wisdom:

1. **Good judgment**. A leader who has wisdom can better handle the challenges that arise from leading. This is because good judgment comes to those who are wise. Wisdom, like good judgment, comes with experience. When you have good judgment you will always be solving problems, seeing better results, and moving forward.
2. **Strong character**. Integrity and character should be the foundation of a leader's life. This starts when you know and follow your Leadership Core. Strong character produces wisdom, which leads to the ability to positively impact others. This is because wise leaders have been through many different experiences and have maintained their integrity through it. If you are intentional in maintaining your character and growing in wisdom, then you will be unstoppable.
3. **It brings honor**. Wisdom brings honor within your personal and professional life. Over time this honor will lead to your Lasting Legacy. When you grow in wisdom, then your honor among others starts to rise. This is because your life is an example of someone worth following.
4. **Grows influence**. Your wisdom will increase your ability to influence others. This is because who you are and what you do attracts like-minded people. Those who have wisdom, talent, and a good track record will want to follow you because of your wisdom. It's like the old saying "Birds of a feather stick together." When you grow and have wisdom, it will increase your reach and influence.

What the Experts Say

Dr. Phyllis Wise, Chancellor of University of Illinois at Urbana-Champaign, explained the impact wisdom has had on her leadership at the university level. She explained:

I have always believed consultation with others who are better than I am in their specific areas is the best way to achieve success for the institution. I believe in choosing people to be on my team who believe in the mission of the institution, who are smarter than I am, collaborative, and willing to work with others on the team. This is where you get the translation of knowledge into actions that benefit your organization. Whether you define this as "wisdom" or not, I'm not entirely sure, but I think this approach of bringing the smartest and broadest range of advice to the table is the difference between making decisions and making the best decisions. It lets you leverage not just your own limited experience, but to harness the collective experiences of many.

For example, when I got to the University of Washington and was the Provost, one of the things I realized on my listening and learning tour was that there were incredible strengths in the broad areas of the environment. But they were spread out, and they were not leveraging each other's strengths and not creating synergies. So, I started consulting with faculty about creating a new College of Environment. A group of respected faculty and I came to the conclusion that combining the College of Forest Resources with the College of Ocean and Fishery Sciences and other departments in the College of Arts and Sciences would create a college that would have greater visibility, impact and respect than separate units and would attract outstanding students and faculty.

Dr. Wise had the wisdom to use her greatest resource—her staff—to create a college program that is one of the strongest in the country.

Jim Kouzes, author of *The Leadership Challenge*, shared his views on wisdom in leadership during our interview by sharing the following:

Over the last four decades of my career I've been very fortunate to have the opportunity to work with some of the most seasoned professionals in leadership and talent development, and among them was Fred Margolis. Fred taught me one lesson in particular that has profoundly influenced most everything I do as an educator.

It happened over dinner one evening in Washington, D.C., when Fred asked me, "What's the best way to learn something?" Since I'd had extensive training and background in experiential learning—and had a personal preference for that approach—I confidently replied: "The best way to learn something is to experience it yourself." "No," Fred responded instantly, as if he'd sensed I was going to give the answer

I did. "The best way to learn something," he said, "is to teach it to somebody else!"

Fred was absolutely right. No matter whether you're a leader or a new recruit, a veteran or a novice, when you are asked to teach something to another person you start to think, study, and prepare from the moment you're asked to take on that role. In the process you become consumed by learning. You know you're on the line. You know you're going to have to perform live in front of others, and you'd better have your stuff down cold.

The lesson that the best way to learn something is to teach it to somebody else has shaped my teaching style more significantly than any other lesson on learning. It's Fred's legacy, and I've been benefiting from it and passing it on ever since dinner that night. It inspires me daily to discover new methods, invent new tools, and design new experiences that will enable others to grow and develop.

What's even more intriguing to me is that in late 2014 I was reading a study in which the researchers found that "compared to learners expecting a test, learners expecting to teach recalled more material correctly ... organized their recall more effectively, and ... had better memory for... more important information." I'm glad science has provided validation for Fred's observation, but he was way ahead of the research.

So I'd say the best way to "Lead with wisdom" is to always be a teacher. Be someone willing to share what you know with others. But be the kind of teacher who is always learning and always willing to be a student. That way you'll always be open to learning from others, including those you teach.

Jim's point about teaching as a great way of leading should really resonate with leaders in the educational field.

Mark Strom, author of *Lead with Wisdom*, shared in an interview with us what he believes are the three keys to leading with wisdom:

- **Character**. No one follows a vision, least of all some bullet points on a slide. People follow a person telling a compelling story backed by a believable and dependable character. It is helpful to understand our personality type, but it matters little compared to growing in character. So what is character? I think all people are magnificent and are broken. We have cause for dignity and for humility. Character, to me, is how we hold these equal and difficult truths about ourselves and others. I am neither more than you, nor less. You may thrill me with your brilliance, and crush me with your betrayal; and I may do the same. How we hold these truths in tension, not as abstract ideas but as our own lived experience is, for me, character.

- **On behalf of**. A dear friend and colleague gave me these three little words many years ago. If we lead, we dream and wonder and plan and act on behalf of others. Yet at every step we risk being distracted. The "on behalf of" may be turned in on itself: on behalf of the system, on behalf of the process, on behalf of the standard, on behalf of the organization, on behalf of our own insecurities, ambitions, and arrogance. Here, then, is a test of character and skill: Can we turn every inward-looking aberration of purpose outward to those for whom our labors are meant to bring life and hope and good sense? It begins and ends in character: in between lie the skills of crafting great questions, animating flagging conversations, drawing out stories, and building relationship.

- **Brilliance**. Every person has brilliance. Few of us know what it is. The clues lie in our stories. To every leader, I say this: find the "brilliance in the room" before you look for "best practice elsewhere." That is leadership: to believe in people, to hold out truthful hope to them, to draw out their stories and help them name their brilliance, and to create the space for them to grow into this brilliance; first for their own joy, and then for its contribution.

Mark's point about finding brilliance in the room before looking for best practices elsewhere could really change the culture of our schools. Imagine teachers being viewed as the experts and empowered to use their strengths to create a world-class school!

David Pennington, president of AASA, believes there are many keys to increasing wisdom and the capacity to lead. As he explained:

> It's Important to have someone to mentor them or someone they trust that they can call and ask questions. Have someone they can reflect with on decisions they make. Not just bad decisions, but good decisions, too. To ask why did you do something a certain way.
>
> But there is no substitute for experience. When you deal with something two or three times, you will handle it better than the first time.

How many decisions does an administrator make during a day? It is more than most people can even imagine. They are dealing with parents, teachers, students, policies, logistics, etc. It takes a while to learn to handle so much as once. It is kind of like shell shock with your first experiences. Each step up on leadership is different. From grade level, to administrator to superintendent, every role brings its own unique challenges. And those of us who are experienced don't do as good of a job sharing with novice leaders. We forget about what it was like to be a first-year leader. We should share stories with them of our experiences, so they understand they aren't in it alone—such as the first time a parent cussed you out, or you made a decision about a friend's child and how they responded to you.

One difference between the corporate world and education is that leaders don't have much free time. They are tied to school and don't have time to interact with others as much. No time to really just sit and talk. I remember when I was starting out that we had time to sit together, then talk. I would meet once a week with other leaders and have coffee and learn from them. I learned some valuable nuggets from those coffee meetings. I learned things like: some decisions can be set aside for a few days. Everything doesn't need to be addressed immediately. On the flip side, there are many decisions which have to be made quickly. Such as students with behavior issues.

Dr. Gina Ikemoto, executive director of New Leaders, shared her thoughts with us during our interview:

Wisdom is essential, however much of it comes from experience and analysis of the experience. The research on leadership preparation—across fields—is clear that leadership development requires not only knowledge, but also job-embedded, authentic practice. We know from research on educational leadership preparation in particular that residency experiences are a characteristic of high-quality preparation. That's why New Leaders designs all of its leadership preparation programs in ways that emphasize the ability to practice and get feedback. Unfortunately most educational leadership preparation programs don't provide enough practice and feedback before people enter the principalship. So, then, what we see happen is that there is a learning curve for first-time school leaders. They have to live through a lot of experience in the first year in order to gain the wisdom.

Rachael Robertson, an Antarctica Expedition Leader, may have had the most unique perspective on leading with wisdom, because when she made mistakes, people could have potentially died. As she explained in our interview,

> Wisdom is incredibly important and yet it's very hard to fast-track. It's the result of years and years of experience and encountering all sorts of situations and managing them with finesse. Interestingly, the Australian Antarctic Division recruits its Station Leaders specifically for leadership experience; for wisdom.
>
> They recognize that in the three months of training you receive they can teach you all the technical aspects of the job—the Antarctic treaty, environmental policy, the safety management system. But what they can't teach you in three months is wisdom, and deep leadership experience. So they specifically recruit for that quality.
>
> I knew nothing about Antarctica when I applied to lead the expedition (I'd been to the snow once on a primary school excursion!), but I had 16 years' leadership experience. That experience, and wisdom, prepared me well for a year on the ice. Because it meant, whenever a novel or ambiguous situation arose, I could trawl back though my years of experience and look for a similar situation I'd encountered. I could then ask myself, "What worked last time?"
>
> I developed wisdom early in my career simply by asking more experienced people how they would have handled a certain scenario. Sometimes their answer was exactly what I had done, but other times they had an alternative response, which I'd promptly store in my mind for future reference.

Finally, as Coach Bobby Bowden, who was one of my (Brad) childhood heroes, expressed, "living a life of principles is missing somewhat in our culture." As he explained:

> We go to college and get knowledge, but without wisdom knowledge is not as effective. This wisdom is based upon values and ethics. These are the basic fundamentals that we need to instill into their children. We have people who don't mind taking shortcuts or doing wrong to get ahead. But, at the end of the day, it is still about being a moral person who thinks of others. Taking shortcuts and compromising your beliefs will never give you long-term success. I always felt like my job as a coach was to teach these young men to be more than just athletes or get them

through school. It was my job to make them better men, to make them men of integrity. I would do Bible studies with the players and I would take to them church during fall camps. I made sure that I not only instilled principles and integrity in my players, but I made sure that I exhibited them in my own life. I wanted the players to see that my beliefs and principles were not just words, but that I lived them too. I always taught that life should be lived by Faith, Family, and Football, and in that order.

Ideas to Try

- **Decisions should be made in terms of values**. Such as, how does this decision affect all the stakeholders, not just one group?
- **Earn your team's respect**. Being a leader means being in command of yourself and your peers. Without either there is no balance. Show compassion and earn the respect of others. Learn to listen and guide.
- **Look for stories**. Stories aren't just great ways to communicate an idea. Stories are how we are wired. Maybe we like neat theories and tidy spreadsheets, but we forget those—we don't forget stories to which we are drawn and connect. Find stories of identity and purpose.
- **Don't presume to know everything**. People need to know you are real and that there may be areas in which you aren't an expert. Competent leaders aren't afraid to say, "I don't know."
- **Recognize the wisdom in others**. This reinforces the strengths-building of your staff. If you only focus on weaknesses, then you will never find out their strengths and wisdom. Their wisdom may be more profound that yours in a particular area.
- **Lead with integrity and character**. As Mark Strom said, people don't follow a mission, or rules, but rather they tend to follow someone they believe in and trust. This also means you should lead with humility.
- **Give**. It is important for us to take the time to give. Whether it is time, money, or our strengths, we should all take the time to help others. Lee Iacocca, one of the top leaders of the 20th Century, believed that all people in positions of power need to give to their communities in some capacity.
- **Be open to new ideas**. A wise leader not is not only open to new ideas, but is looking for them and looking for people who can help provide them.

- **Grow your influence.** Making wise decisions will help you develop trust with those you lead. This will increase your ability to influence others as well, which is what leadership is all about at its core. This influence will help you be a world-class leader!
- **Listen.** Listen more than you speak. Larry King once said that he learns new things from listening not from speaking. Many effective leaders will sit in a meeting and never speak or wait to speak. They listen, listen, and listen!
- **Respond, don't react.** As we have mentioned in other sections, responding to a situation requires conscious thought, not just an emotional response. This requires a level of maturity and wisdom to think things through, even in a tough situation.

Key Points to Remember: Leading with Wisdom

- Lead with character and integrity.
- Give. Help others in some capacity.
- Recognize the wisdom in others.
- Don't act like you know it all.
- Lead with humility.
- Grow your influence.
- Be world-class.
- Listen more than you speak.
- Respond to situations rather than react.

Becoming Resilient and Persevering

"If we are resilient, we will thrive."

Julie Sessions

Resilience and perseverance are like two pieces to a puzzle. They fit and work together, yet they are not the same. Being resilient is the ability to overcome challenges and be strengthened by the outcome. This is a learned and teachable behavior. Perseverance is the will to not give up, and try again and again. Resilience and perseverance often are needed in a time of adversity or change. Adversity builds character, but it also reveals character. What type of character will you have when you have to face changes or adversity? Will you teach others how to persevere and will you help them learn how to be resilient? The level of success experienced is often measured by hard work and resilience.

Here are a common list of traits that go along with both perseverance and resilience. How would you answer some of these questions? Knowing yourself and how you react is a vital aspect of being able to model resilience and perseverance.

- **Struggle**: How do you react when you are struggling with a concept? Are you emotional? Do you get frustrated? Do you make a plan to succeed? Do you let people know it is OK to struggle? Do you provide or seek help and support?
- **Self-efficacy**: Do you believe in yourself? Do you often give up on yourself and want to quit or pass the task on to others? How do you feel about yourself? What do you think of yourself? Do you view problems and goals to be mastered? Do you recover quickly from setbacks or failures?

- **Ability to adapt**: Do you adapt well to change? Do you go with the flow? Do you get emotionally attached? Can you separate personal from professional? Are you willing to listen to others and work as a team to succeed? Do you focus on the past?
- **Stamina**: Do you get tired easily? Are you easily frustrated? Do you feel like you want to give up? Do you look at each new day as a fresh start? Are you encouraging to others? Do you have willpower? Have you experienced the feeling of a "runner's high," like you can go on forever? Do you know what it means to push on?
- **Character traits and virtues**: Are you aware of your own character traits and the traits you value in others? Are you kind? Are you caring? Are you patient? Do you promote respect? Are you thankful? Do you encourage excellence? Do you encourage cooperation? Are you a good listener?
- **Modeling**: What do you model to your employees or people who work with and for you? Are you a planner? Can you make decisions? Do you have the ability to bounce back? Are you resourceful? Do you encourage critical thinking and creativity? Do you promote growth?

Schools are safe environments that can promote a culture of resilience. This is true for the faculty, staff, administration, and the students. The faculty and staff will learn resiliency traits and experience success with resilience when you as a leader model and teach those traits. By giving them tasks and helping with this learned skill, you can create a culture of resilience. This can then be transferred into the classroom. Once the faculty and staff have these skills, then they can teach them to the students. Besides family, schools are the place where children feel most safe and can develop relationships that will foster resilience. Schools provide a social and emotional wellbeing along with a large support system. Resilience is a lifelong skill that can be transferred into almost any aspect of life.

What the Experts Say

We feel that opening this section with a couple of quotes is appropriate and will hopefully make you think. Confucius states, "Our greatest glory is not in never falling, but in rising every time we fall." Thomas Edison says, "I haven't failed. I've identified 10,000 ways this doesn't work." Two great men who led the world and inspired millions both exude the qualities of perseverance and resilience.

According to *The Resilient Leader*, by Elle Allison (2011/2012), there are characteristics and key points of research that describe resilience traits. There are also aspects of risk that will hinder resilience if done within a work environment.

Characteristics of Resilience

- being able to bounce back
- the ability to manage emotions
- being aware of strengths and assets
- having a passion-driven focus
- recognizing and maintaining problem-solving skills
- being resourceful
- having a sense of personal agency
- having the ability to reach out to others

Key Points from Resilience Research

- All individuals have the power to transform and change.
- Teachers and schools have the power to transform lives.
- It's how teachers do what they do that counts.
- Teachers' beliefs in innate capacity start the change process.

Risks That Will Hinder Resilience

- **Stopping your Learning.** Any time anyone in a leadership position stops learning, then problems can occur. On the surface it shows a lack of caring or lack of initiative. The willingness to learn equates with the willingness to grow, which ultimately means not giving up. It is fine if leaders delegate research and learning opportunities to others on their team, but it is essential the leaders are also willing to continually learn.
- **Having too many tasks.** Take it one step at a time. Getting bogged down with numerous tasks can be daunting and exhausting. Be able

to prioritize and share the workload. Give people a break in between tasks before jumping into the next best thing. People will get worn out and not want to put forth the time and effort to support you as a leader. They will never be able to learn the feeling and success of being resilient if there are several different aspects they are working on at one time. Stick to one, finish it, and then move on when the time is right.

- **Forgetting to Reflect and Even Celebrate Success.** While it is understandable that you want to move on to the next task, it is essential that you fully have closure on the task that was just completed. Yes, it takes time, but reflection is a key aspect to any job. Going over the pros and cons, and learning from both, is critical. People often consider this one of the most important phases of a project. Taking what we learn from one project can definitely help the next. Celebration is also important. Take time to compliment yourself and others who successfully completed the task. This positive reinforcement helps the mental states of the workers as well as builds morale.
- **Don't blame.** It is easy to blame someone or something, but be careful. Wrongly blaming can be a problem within itself. This can break down teams and deter from the task at hand. Blaming something general like the budget or upper administration is also a cop-out. Stay away from blame, and focus on how to succeed. Blaming is an excuse of why something will not get done and takes a negative tone. Stay positive and persevere.

Christina Parker, Executive Director of Georgia Association on Young Children (GAYC) shares her thoughts on resiliency and perseverance and the importance it plays in leadership roles and in life in general.

Resiliency, "the ability to bounce back when problems arise," is a very important trait for everyone, not just a leader. Life is constantly changing and evolving in our personal life as well as our professional life and one of my sayings is "innovate or die." I believe that problems and setbacks will always occur and those with resilience and perseverance are more likely to be able to change their perspective when problems arise to one of a positive nature. One of my biggest examples of resiliency and leadership is when we purchased the Bruster's Franchise. It was in the bottom performers of the chain and we had a choice:

continue to do things the way they had always been done and stay in the bottom performers, or look at things differently and change it up. We chose to be resilient and change the way of operations and strove for better. The results soon followed. Shortly after climbing back to the top of the chain in performance, I was diagnosed with Stage 3 breast cancer that doctors said could take my life in six months. I could have given up then, but decided once again to be resilient and lean on the leaders that we had developed within the store to continue running and growing the business. The business continued to flourish and that was when I started to realize my leadership muscle and what traits helped people want to perform. Not because they had to, but because as a leader you had developed and invested in them personally and they wanted to.

Resilience Training International (RTI) founder Glenn Schiraldi explains that resilience is defined as those strengths of mind and character, both innate and developed, which enable us to adapt well to adversity. According to Schiraldi, resilience helps ups to survive and rebound from difficult times, improve and maintain mental fitness and performance under pressure, transform negative moods, and increase happiness and enjoyment throughout our lives (http://resiliencefirst.com/index.html).

Rachael Robertson, Antarctic Expedition Leader, leadership expert, author, speaker, and mentor, states that she believes the two most important traits in a leader are self-awareness and resilience. She shares the following:

> A large part of self-awareness is knowing how your words, actions, and body language impact the people around you. It's understanding that when things go pear-shaped people look to the leader for reassurance and guidance, so you need to remain optimistic, calm, poised, and confident—even if you don't feel that! Self-awareness is also knowing what you're good at and knowing when you need to call in extra expertise from the people around you.
>
> The best leaders I've worked with are all incredibly self-aware and they work hard on building this quality. While many people are born with a natural ability to critically analyze themselves and their performance, it can also be learned. The best way to develop self-awareness is through reflection. Stepping back at the end of each day and asking yourself, "How did I handle that?" "Did I get the outcome I expected?" "Could I have done it better?" In Antarctica, where I led a team of

18 people for a year, I had no peers or mentors to guide me, so the only way I knew if I was doing something correctly, or not, was to reflect each day by writing in a journal. Psychometric tests and frank feedback from a trusted peer are also incredibly useful. Resilience is also very important for leaders. You need to be able to bounce back from disappointment. This is also a learned behavior—and it starts at a very young age. My schoolteachers were fundamental in helping me to learn that I won't always win, I won't always get things right—and that's OK. It built a foundation for my adult life and the strong self-belief that I could, and would, overcome adversity. That poise and optimism is critical for leadership.

Ideas to Try

- **Try professional training.** Resilience training is an option for helping learn approaches and traits for being resilient. This is an alternative type of training that focuses on being prepared and not reactive, but prepared. This can be used to help prepare for crisis situations, but also to just promote a culture of resilience within your workplace. Here is a site that can give you further information: http://resiliencefirst.com/training.html

- **Practice arousal reduction.** Practicing arousal reduction can help with reactions when stressful situations occur. This can be done for yourself or for your entire team. These include heartrate and performance-calming skills, breathing, yoga, relaxation, and ways to promote calm thinking.

- **Learn to handle negative emotions.** There are ways to de-stress your negative emotions or emotions that may take away from attaining the goal. These emotions can include anger, fear, sadness, guilt, and grief. Have a plan in place to handle these emotions when they arise. This may be having a support system, such as a guidance counselor or support group. It can be keeping a journal or having an emotional-exercise release group. The importance is recognizing these emotions will occur and having a way to de-stress the emotions.

- **Promote happiness.** A happy working environment is a healthy working environment. Find ways to promote happiness. This may include humor or breaks for fun. Giving little awards or recognitions, playing games, taking breaks for goofy things, and allowing for silliness is healthy and needed for positive morale. While it may seem like a waste of time and money, the benefits of positive attitudes and willingness to persevere will far exceed the costs.

- **Don't quit**. There are times and situations where you may want to quit, give up, or stop working on a task or goal. Don't quit. See it through. The people working for you need to see and experience closure. This may mean formally stating that it is no longer a focus, but give reasons why and give closure to the project. Quitting something means to leave it hanging and unresolved. Modeling this will model that you do not value being resilient or perseverance.

- **Set goals**. Everyone should have goals, whether they are personal and/or professional. Support and value these goals. Model that you have goals of your own. By everyone having goals to aspire to, you can all work on the process together. Make plans, document steps, have a support system, modify and adjust the goals if needed, and then reflect. The goal-setting process gives a personal connection with learning how to persevere and be resilient. Once people personally relate with the process, then it is more likely to be carried over to the workplace.

- **Fight for it**. When you lead you are asking a lot of your workers in respect to taking on tasks and responsibility. Be sure to communicate your goals and expectations to your faculty and staff and be willing to fight for what you want. This includes having a plan, doing the research, and being able to justify the plan. This also includes being willing to *fight for them*. Your workers are your support system. You have to fight for what they want in regards to change. Always think of the growth, but not just your own. If someone wants to change a position or work on a different task, be supportive and consider the overall growth that will come out of the change.

- **Look ahead**. Every new thing creates another new thing and new opportunities. Accept your new reality and be willing to move on. Dwelling on the past will do nothing in regards to growth. Learn from the past, but do not dwell. Looking ahead also means to be proactive. Make connections from one task to another and try to plan ahead to see where it will take you.

Key Points to Remember: Becoming Resilient and Persevering

- Resilience and perseverance are not the same, but are both key aspects in reaching goals and showing growth
- Be proactive and help teach your faculty and staff about being resilient.
- Have a large support staff available.
- Practice goal-setting and experience resilience and persevering with your faculty and staff.
- Promote a culture of respect.

Key 11 — Lead with EQ vs. IQ

The Art of Leadership is all about self-awareness and relating to others.
Brad Johnson

In the past, leadership has been seen as something of power, intellect, and even fear. Think of men of the past who were voted as successful leaders in a magazine. These were people seen as tough, demanding, and powerful. However, over the past few decades, research has shown that the most effective leaders are not these demanding, dictator-like bosses that we see in some movies or even reality shows. Rather, effective leadership is more about what used to be termed as soft skills, but maybe now they should be coined essential skills. These are the traits known as EQ (emotional intelligence).

There are five domains that deal with EQ that are important to effective leadership. Leadership is not just about what you know, but understanding how to relate to others, inspire them and help them be successful. The five domains to the EQ of leadership include: self-awareness, self-regulation (control), empathy, motivation, and social skills. Below are brief descriptions of each domain as described in *What is Emotional Intelligence (EQ)?* (Akers & Porter, 2007).

1. **Self-awareness**. The ability to recognize an emotion as it "happens" is the key to your EQ. If you evaluate your emotions, you can manage them. The major elements of self-awareness are emotional awareness and self-confidence.
2. **Self-regulation**. You often have little control over when you experience emotions. You can, however, have some say in how long an emotion

will last by using a number of techniques to alleviate negative emotions such as anger, anxiety, or depression. A few of these techniques include: recasting a situation in a more positive light, taking a long walk, and meditation or prayer. Self-regulation involves traits such as self-control, trustworthiness, conscientiousness, and adaptability.

3. **Motivation.** To motivate yourself for any achievement requires clear goals and a positive attitude. Although you may have a predisposition to either a positive or a negative attitude, you can with effort and practice learn to think more positively. If you catch negative thoughts as they occur, you can reframe them in more positive terms—which will help you achieve your goals. Motivation is made up of achievement, commitment, and optimism.

4. **Empathy.** This is the ability to recognize how people feel is important to success in your life and career. The more skillful you are at discerning the feelings behind others' signals, the better you can control the signals you send them. An empathetic person excels at service orientation, developing others, and understanding others.

5. **Social skills.** The development of good interpersonal skills is paramount to success in your life and career. In today's always-connected world, everyone has immediate access to technical knowledge. Thus, "people skills" are even more important now, because you must possess a high EQ to better understand, empathize, and negotiate with others in a global economy. Among the most useful skills are influence, communication, conflict management, and collaboration.

A high degree of emotional intelligence has personal benefits. For example, increased self-awareness helps you respond better to day-to-day situations you face personally and professionally, such as a personnel issue or even road rage on the way home from work. In the same cases, a heightened level of empathy can help reduce the duration of these episodes and can lead to a healthier response from the other parties.

Emotional intelligence also translates to optimal outcomes as a leader. In challenging situations such as negotiations and terminations, or even in positive cases such as celebrations or achievements, a high degree of EQ can go a long way in building strong relationships and cementing your role as an effective leader.

People without the skills may not be the most socially adept. Have you ever met people who were very intelligent but couldn't seem to relate to people or who you might describe as socially awkward? These are people who may exhibit low EQ and it may hinder them from being effective leaders. Interestingly, most people assume that teachers have high EQ because they care about children, focus on developing relationships, and often have good interpersonal skills. But when moving into a leadership role, is there a change in social interaction, self-awareness, and the importance of maintaining relationships?

EQ is not only important as a teacher, but it is important as an administrator/leader. In fact, it may be even more important as a leader because leaders set the tone for the culture of the school. As we mentioned in Key 6, culture influences an organization more than policies and rules, but it is leadership that influences the culture. So when leaders are self-aware, have great people skills, are empathetic, and know how to focus on strengths of staff to motivate them, then these leaders create a school culture that is world-class.

Research by EQ experts like **Travis Bradberry** suggests that transformational leadership has many similar traits of leaders with high EQ. He also says that the place that leaders struggle the most is in self-awareness—understanding how people see them and what they really look like from the outside. So, let's examine the importance of EQ according to some of the leading experts on the topic.

What the Experts Say

Sally Helgesen, leadership expert, explained,

> EQ is important and becoming more important every passing year. Demands of organizations are becoming more intense and people are being asked to perform at higher levels. We now are competing in a global market. In the public schools, such things as government oversight makes it difficult for people to perform well. The urgency and greater need to emphasize innovation and creativity is more important than before for leaders to be able to engage people at both a broad and deep level. You can't do this without EQ and the ability to empathize with the people you lead.

Travis Bradberry is considered one of the leading experts in EQ around the globe. He took the time to share his expertise with us on the subject. As he explained:

> The place that leaders struggle the most is in self-awareness—understanding how people see them and what they really look like

from the outside. Most of us are putting the blinders on and not taking a look at the things that we need to change because we think it isn't going to do us any good. EQ doesn't work this way. We need to be self-aware. When you discover what you need to be doing differently, what you're poor at, that's what opens the door to improved performance. So self-awareness is key. You have to know what it is you need to do, and once you do it's very powerful. I have had many people come to me and say how empowering it is for them to understand all this stuff that they had no clue they were doing over the years, and how much it has really just sort of pushed their performance to new heights in leadership roles.

Emotional intelligence is a foundational skill, and emotions are the primary driver of our behavior. Pick a skill and a behavior that you're going to practice. Actually, after you take the test that comes with my book, *Emotional Intelligence 2.0*, the report will tell you specifically what EQ skills you ought to start practicing, and how. You need to practice these new behaviors to make it habitual. The first time you try to do it, your brain isn't going to like it. It's very difficult to do the first time, the first five times, the first 10 times, but your brain loves efficiency. It loves it. It wants to make behaviors easy.

Unlike IQ—which is fixed—EQ can be developed throughout your lifespan. Your IQ is the same at age 5 as it is at age 50. Emotional intelligence is a flexible skill, and is something that you can work on. You can physically change your brain. There's a neuronal pathway between the rational and emotional centers of your brain. When you work on your EQ you actually build new neurons, you grow new pathways, or you advance the pathway that increases the flow of information.

There's a very high threshold of IQ in leadership positions. You're self-selected to be above average intelligence. All your competitors and your peers are swimming in the same boat. Therefore, IQ becomes less of a predictor of your success when the playing field is level. Actually, people are weeded out based on their IQ at this point. The question to ask then is what is that thing that distinguishes these high-IQ leaders. Often emotional intelligence becomes a very important indicator of performance. In my research, I've found that 90% of top performers in leadership positions are high in emotional intelligence, whereas only 20% of bottom performers are high in emotional intelligence. EQ isn't a guarantee of success, but there's a massive correlation between EQ and performance. It's about as close as you're going to get.

In fact, a few years back, my company, TalentSmart, partnered with the University of South Africa—School of Business Management to conduct such a study. Data were collected from 314 close associates of the managers, including their managers, peers, and subordinates, by using our Emotional Intelligence Appraisal and the Multifactor Leadership Questionnaire (MLQ) Form 5X. The results showed a positive correlation between all the emotional intelligence subscales and all the transformational leadership subscales. The results of this study support those of other international studies, suggesting a positive relationship between emotional intelligence and transformational leadership.

Dan Domenech, executive director of AASA, shared that EQ is very important in effective leadership. He shared:

I often tell story where Eisenhower describes leadership as a piece of string. If you push it, then it makes a mess, but if you get in front and pull it, then they will follow you. You can't push people to follow, but you lead by example, motivate, they trust and are loyal to you. Convince people that your vision is the correct vision. They will want to follow you. Those without high EQ have to coerce people into following them, but they aren't very effective and don't last long as a leader.

When we asked **Fawn Germer**, author of *Hard Won Wisdom*, about the importance of emotional intelligence over IQ, she explained, "You learned everything you need to know about leadership in elementary school. Don't push in line. Listen. Respect other people's opinions. Admit your mistakes. Keep your promises. Tell the truth. It goes on and on. You don't need to read a 400 page book on being a good leader. You need to look within and see how others have inspired you to follow them. Usually, it is by having a good, clear vision and treating people well."

Dr. Gina Ikemoto, New Leaders' Director, believes that EQ is highly important! As she explained,

We have found that these skills make or break a principal, particularly in the first year. Without self-awareness we often create or build problems—and we do not understand our impact on others. An effective leader successfully champions their vision and creates school cultures that thrive. If leaders are not confident in their abilities, if they do not understand their weaknesses, then there will be little impact on others. It is very important for school leaders to be change agents and team-builders. Personal leadership is tricky because it is a disposition; however, personal leadership can be developed. That's why we at New Leaders emphasize these skills in our selection process but also provide explicit training and development. It is also the reason that we decided to create our Emerging Leaders program for teacher leaders. We wanted to provide teacher leaders with more time and opportunities to practice and grow these personal leadership skills before entering our Aspiring Principals Program.

Finally, Mike Abrashoff shared in our interview the difference between himself and the captain he was relieving on the USS *Benfold*. As Mike recounts to us and in his book, *It's Your Ship*,

> The former commander was a very intelligent man and he ran a tight ship as far as making sure things were clean, duties completed, etc. However, he lacked in personal skills or developing relationships with the crew. He treated them more like children than adults. When I took control of the ship, it seemed like the whole crew was demoralized and they actually cheered as the former commander left the ship.
>
> I knew in that moment that I had to bring a different approach to leadership. So, I had two goals in mind as I took over command of the ship. First is that there are always better ways of doing things and that maybe the crew's insight may be even more profound than the captain's. So, I spent months asking the crew if there is a better way to do their job. Secondly, I focused on encouraging the crew to not only find more effective ways to do their job but to have fun doing it.

Focusing on the crew, empowering them, and creating a fun working culture where possible are all reflective of a leader who is self-aware, and utilizing emotional intelligence to get the most out of themselves and their crew.

Ideas to Try

- **Take an EQ or emotional intelligence assessment**. EQ 2.0 is an assessment that will identify your top emotional intelligence traits. This will help you identify the traits you possess that are your strengths. From here you will be able to continue to develop those strengths and use them to become a more effective leader.

- **Be aware of emotions**. Just becoming aware of your emotions can help raise your EQ. Stop periodically throughout your day to assess what and how you are feeling. Set a timer for various points during the day. When the timer goes off, take a few deep breaths and notice how you're feeling emotionally. Pay attention to where that emotion is showing up as a physical feeling in your body and what the sensation feels like.

- **Embrace your EQ**. Instead of shutting emotions down, try to embrace them. Learn how to use them to your advantage. Remember: they will benefit you personally and professionally. Keeping a journal or making mental notes of when you are using your emotions will help you to reflect back on the process.

- **Read people's body language**. Make a point of trying to read between the lines and pick up on people's true feelings by observing their facial expressions and other body language. We speak more with our bodies than with our words! Be sure to take that all in before, and even while, you are communicating.

- **Be aware of your behavior**. Notice how you act when you're experiencing certain emotions, and how that affects your day-to-day life. Does it impact your communication with others, your productivity, or your overall sense of wellbeing?

- **Practice responding, rather than reacting**. Reacting is an unconscious process where we experience an emotional trigger, but responding is a conscious process that involves noticing how you feel, then deciding how you want to behave.

- **Have an attitude of gratitude**. Make time to notice what is going well and where you feel grateful in your life. Creating a positive environment not only improves your quality of life, but it can be contagious to people around you, too. Verbalize the gratitude, or make it known to yourself or others.

- **Pay attention to your body**. Our minds and bodies are not separate; they affect each other quite deeply. You can raise your EQ by learning how to read physical cues that clue you in to what emotions you're feeling. Stress might feel like a knot in your stomach, tight chest, or quick breathing. Sadness might feel like waking up with slow, heavy limbs. Joy or pleasure might feel like butterflies in your stomach, a racing heart, or increased energy.

- **Be open-minded and agreeable**. Openness and being agreeable go hand-in-hand when it comes to emotional intelligence. A narrow mind is generally an indication of a lower EQ. When your mind is open through understanding and internal reflection, it becomes easier to deal with conflicts in a calm and self-assured manner. You will find yourself socially aware and new possibilities will be open to you.
- **Practice being emotionally honest**. If you say you're "fine" and have a scowl on your face, you're not communicating honestly. Practice being more physically open with your emotions, so people can read you better. Tell people when you're upset, and share happiness and joy as well.
- **Laugh often**. Beyond gratitude, find and use humor when possible. People with high EQ tend to know how to use fun and humor to make themselves and others feel safer and happier. Use laughter to get through tough times.

Key Points to Remember: Leading with EQ

- Embrace your EQ—these aren't soft skills but essential skills.
- Reflect on your EQ during the day.
- Learn to respond rather than react.
- Keep an attitude of gratitude.
- Use humor as often as possible.
- Be open-minded.
- Be other-focused.

Key 12 | Balance Your Personal and Professional Life

"A balanced life is a both productive and fulfilling life."

Brad Johnson

The dynamics of our work environment have changed. Work used to take place at a specific location for a certain numbers of hours in the day. Then you would leave, go home, and have separation from work. Essentially you would leave the work at the office and have personal time when home. That is no longer the case and that is mostly due to advances in technology as well as working in a borderless, global society. The 9:00 A.M to 5:00 P.M. job no longer exists. Thanks to technology, conference calls and collaborative work occurs all over the world at all hours of the day and night. There has been a cultural shift. Whether it is due to having a good work ethic, being competitive, or striving to advance in your career, turning work off is becoming harder and harder. Have we lost the balance?

It seems that the professional and personal environments have become blended. We allow one to seep into the other and unfortunately impact the other. We live in a world where it is acceptable to have cell phones at the dinner table and work at home. We let professional time interfere with personal time. But we also ask for daycares at work and miss important meetings and deadlines due to personal reasons. We let our personal lives impact our professional lives. How do we balance this? Should we keep them separate? Which one would you value as more important: personal or professional? Why do we view one as more important than the other?

Is it Balance or Integration?

Some people think balance is a myth and it can never truly occur. Balance implies that equal time and effort is given to each separately. Can you really equally split time and balance the effort you give, both emotionally and physically, to both home and work? Some people say they can, while others say one seems to win out and the other gets ignored. Balance also means that at times one needs, or gets, more attention than the other, but then eventually this switches to the other aspect receiving the attention. The goal is to be equal with the amount of time and effort given to both aspects. Does this mean while at work you focus 100% on the job and while you are at home you focus 100% on your home life? In this day and age with technology, is that even possible?

Integrating means that one can flow into another and each is a part of the other. There are people who prefer this and even enjoy the mix, but others think they should be compartmentalized. Should there be daycares at work? Some like that there is childcare available, but there are others who say that they feel like they stay longer at work because they don't have to leave to pick up the kids. What about checking emails or working on projects at home? Some people say if that is how they choose to spend their free time, then so be it. They also point out that at least they are with family or friends and not stuck in the office. Others say there needs to be a limit to the integration.

So, is it a balance or is it integration? They answer is both. You need to find a balance in the way you integrate your personal and professional life. If you do not find this balance on how to successfully integrate both personal and professional lives, there can be serious consequences. Here are just a few:

- **Impact on health**. Getting run-down, sickness, obesity, stress disorders, cancer, heart disease, depression, and more.
- **Impact on relationships**. Termination of relationships, missing out on special events, lack of connection with those who matter.
- **Stunting self-growth and losing passion**. You should continue to grow both personally and professionally. Not doing so may lead to quitting or being terminated. It will harm your self-esteem and how you feel about your self-worth. You should grow professionally and continue to learn and be passionate about your career. You should grow personally and be passionate about things in your life.

Who Supports You and Whom Do You Support?

Knowing your roles and responsibilities in your life is really where you should start. Who is your support team? Do you have a family at home who can pick up the slack if you are not able to be there? What about at work? Do those in your personal life support your personal and professional goals? Do those in your professional life support your personal and professional goals? Are they willing to help you achieve your goals? Do you have kids or parents in need? Are you the only caregiver? Are you in a new relationship? What responsibilities do you have at home? What about at work? As you go to answer questions like this, you will realize that you need support. So, who is there to support you and whom do you support?

The *Harvard Business Review* conducted a study covering five years of interviews with almost 4,000 executives worldwide. Here are some facts about balancing personal and professional lives. Note the gender differences.

- 88% of men are married and 60% of those have spouses that do not work full-time outside of the home. 70% of women are married and 10% of those have spouses that do not work fulltime outside of the home.
- Men view themselves as working for their families and claim responsibility in terms of breadwinning, whereas women see themselves as role models for their children.
- Male executives admitted that they don't prioritize their families enough. And women are more likely than men to have foregone kids or marriage to avoid the pressures of combining work and family.
- Both men and women expressed versions of this guilt and associated personal success with not having regrets.

What the Experts Say

Dianna Booher, leadership expert, shared in our interview:

> My philosophy has not been to balance professional and personal life, but to combine them creatively. In today's culture and fast-paced living, work and professional life can no longer be compartmentalized so that you have four hours here and six hours there or three days on and two days off. As a leader, your job is to combine responsibilities for

all roles you play 24/7. That means that the skills, techniques, values, and characteristics you develop in your life must be integrated in your lifestyle, personality, and thinking so that they become innate to the way you handle people, make decisions, and manage time in all situations. Leadership becomes the way you approach life—whether at work or at play.

Fawn Germer, leadership expert, explained:

balance is such a huge issue—for women and men ... for parents and people with and without children. The question is: How can you achieve an inner equilibrium when there are so many outside forces demanding your time? The answer is: You make tough choices. It really is not about balance. It is about knowing your priorities and honoring them. I learned this lesson early on in my career. I wrote down my life priorities in order, with God and family at the top, then physical activity, creativity, work, adventure, nature, community, service, etc. following after. Work was getting 90% of my time. Well, life flies by. If you don't set boundaries and honor what truly matters to you, you aren't living your life. You are living somebody else's life. If your job doesn't let you have a life, you are in the wrong job. I do a lot of work with this and it amazes me how the life balance question is absolutely universal around the world.

Leadership expert Sally Helgesen shared that, rather than balance personal and professional life, that she focuses on integrating them:

I try to integrate my personal and work lives rather than "balance" them. What this looks like for me is developing very close personal relationships with colleagues that give me inspiration and a profound level of support and connectedness while serving as a sounding board for me (as I do for them) when things are difficult.

The other side of this is engaging family members and personal friends whose relationship with me is not rooted in work in talking through work challenges—great ideas come from surprising places—and including them in work activities, i.e., taking my old college roommate along on a trip to Deauville, France, where I was speaking, and finding a role for her to play that expanded her horizons beyond her usual social worker role. This integration makes me feel supported—when I have a stumbling block, my first response is always, "Who I can call?"

I have also benefited by making sure that the texture of my everyday at home satisfies my need for domesticity. When I lived in NYC, my apartment, while enormously convenient, often felt like the hotel rooms where I spent an enormous amount of my time. Since I moved to an old farmhouse in the country and invited some animal friends into my life, the contrast is stunning and gives me a feeling of inherent balance. Of course, I can do this in part because my husband doesn't travel for work and so is able to keep things on track—and because I have a husband in the first place.

To me, being fired with a sense of mission and purpose in life is rather surprisingly the secret to balance—it helps you know what to pursue and what not to pursue and so serves an essential sense of wholeness. Finally, I strive to be as present as possible for every situation—for the person I am talking with, the program I am developing or delivering, the project I am working on, the walk I am taking. This is fundamental to a sense of balance, as the human mind achieves its greatest sense of harmony (and thus balance) when doing one thing at a time.

I believe this big picture approach is helpful, though it works out in different ways depending on what stage you're at in life and what responsibilities you have to bear. But dividing your life up into compartments and trying to calibrate how much to allocate to each is surely not the smoothest path.

Finally, Rachael Robertson, Antarctica Expedition Leader, explained how she balances her life, which can be quite hectic at times:

What works for me is managing my personal boundaries and not being available to every person, all the time—that's exhausting and wears you out. To be able to manage all aspects of life requires resilience and energy and sometimes that means saying "Not now." When you're trying to balance work, home, community, and health, you need to make sure you keep some energy in your tank.

The desire to respond immediately to enquiries and requests from other people is as natural as it is constant. For most of us it's about being supportive and encouraging. We want to be helpful and provide clear direction and advice. However, when these interactions become interruptions, (particularly at work) and our stress levels rise at the thought of the mountain of other work still needing our attention as we respond to this new request, it actually becomes a problem. We can be distracted, sometimes anxious, and it becomes difficult to focus and be fully engaged in the conversation—to actually listen, not just hear, what is being said.

Managing personal boundaries requires the judgment to be **selectively available**. It means having the self-awareness and professionalism to be fully listening and engaged with the right person, at the right time. It's not about saying, "No." It's not about delegating. These are different issues. It's about you managing your time, workload, and other people's expectations to optimize your performance, be highly effective, and look after yourself.

Selective availability is about **flipping the interaction** so that the person seeking you out knows it is absolutely in their best interest to meet with you at the optimal time. It is what is best for them—not you.

For example:

Them: Hi, Rachael. Have you got five minutes to discuss the agenda for the meeting next week?

Me: Actually I don't right now. I have a deadline to get this report to the Business Manager by 3pm. But I really want to hear your thoughts on this because it's important, so how about you come back at.. say 3:30pm and we can go through it then in detail?

The message is: if you can meet with me at the arranged time of 3:30 p.m., rather than discuss this spontaneously right now, you will have my full, undivided attention and considered response. This is what's best for *you*; it's not just about me.

A similar technique is effective if you have been asked to make a decision on the spot but don't feel you have the appropriate data, background or information to make a considered decision. It's not about saying, "No"; it's about saying, "Not now." Being selectively available requires three things:

1. **Judgment**. Know what is important and urgent and therefore needs your attention immediately, and what doesn't.
2. **Self-awareness** – know your emotional responses and, if "now is not the right time," say so. Be firm, gracious, and direct.
3. **Empathy**. (Most) people—besides small children!—won't interrupt you if they can see you are concentrating, unless they feel they really need to. Be sensitive, but firm, in managing the interaction. If faced with

resistance, repeat your statement or request. It's not about saying, "No"; it's about saying "Not now."

Rachel brings up a critical point for leaders and that is to make the most of your time. Responding with a "not now" rather than a "no" respects your time, and meeting later shows that you respect their need to meet. It is a "win-win."

Ideas to Try

- **Rethink how you work**. Are you organized and focused while at work? Do you give 100% at work and do you give 100% at home? Rethinking how you work can help with trying to manage having both a successful personal and professional life.

- **Manage technology**. Make rules and stick by them. Are there technology-free times when you are totally disconnected? Communicate this with both your coworkers and your family. Stick to it the best that you can.

- **Support groups and networking**. Know your support group. This could be family, friends, paid help, or anyone who can assist you in a time of need. This does include professional help. This includes emotional support and well as tactile support. If someone cleans your house enabling you to have more time with the children, then so be it. If you need to get professional help for managing stress, then so be it. Knowing who to go to when you need help is important to being able to have a successful professional and personal life.

- **Professional training**. There are a lot of professional training opportunities available to help with learning how to balance and integrate your personal and professional help. There are workshops as well as courses. One that we looked at was http://www.worklifebalance.com

- **Go off the grid**. This means totally unplug and separate one aspect from the other. This may mean that this is personal time or family time—you decide—but it also means you do not mix business with personal. Make sure you have a support team in place to take over while you are gone. Trust that things can go on without you, and go off the grid. Personal relaxation is a must.

- **Set your priorities**. Make a list of your priorities and then use that as a guide for how you want to let one aspect cross into another. If a goal or priority is to be promoted, then maybe work takes precedence over personal. If a goal is to not miss a child's soccer game, then make that happen. Priorities can change and your list should evolve. But start by making the list first and recognizing what you deem most important in your life.

- **Be 100% in the moment**. During the times that matter, be 100% in the moment. If a major presentation is happening, be sure to let your family know it is not a time to be contacting work, if possible. If you are watching a school performance, do not have your cell phone on buzzing every time someone emails you. This cannot always happen, so designate these special times. Communicate the importance of the events, and be 100% in the moment.
- **Schedule alone time**. Having time to yourself can be peaceful. This can happen at work and at home. This self-reflection time can help with giving you renewed energy. Taking a moment for yourself is essential, because often you will feel like you give your time to everyone else.
- **Stress releasers**. Find stress releasers such as exercise, yoga, massages, skydiving, new hobbies, etc. This is personal time. Find new passions or try new things. Open your mind to learning something new or going someplace you have never been. The emotional journey is as important as the intellectual journey that can accompany the activity you partake in to release stress.
- **Not now**. Rather than simply saying "No" to a request, or even saying "Yes" when you really don't have the time, simply offer another time when someone can then have your full attention.

Key Points to Remember: Balancing Your Personal and Professional Life

- Make a list of priorities.
- Make a list of goals.
- Know your support team.
- Accept you will have to balance and integrate personal and professional lives.
- Follow your passions.
- Take alone-time.
- Follow the "not now" advice.

Be Flexible, Adaptable, and Creative

"If you are not flexible, you may just break."

Julie Sessions

As a leader, one thing you can count on is change. It may be a change in staffing, a change in policy, or a change in procedures. The changes can be major or minor. They can be long-range and expected, or can be on a moment's notice. The possibilities are limitless and one thing you can count on is that change is inevitable. How you react to change will define you as a leader. Are you going to be a facilitator of change? Are you flexible and willing to change when needed? Can you adapt to changes that occur? Are you creative with your planning and generating ways to adapt? These are all qualities that make an effective leader. Being a leader does not mean you will just survive the change, but that you will show growth from the change and welcome continual change.

Flexibility, adaptability, and creativity are aspects that are vital in regards to change. These qualities will help the change to be successful and productive. Leaders at every level should recognize the importance of these qualities and promote a culture that not only respects but also welcomes change.

Flexibility

Being flexible is often very challenging. We tend to have gut reactions that show we are not welcome to change and give the impression we are not flexible. You often cannot control the change that will occur, but how you react can be controlled. Giving the impression that you are flexible is a key leadership skill. You may be emotional on the inside, but there are appropriate audiences in which to share that. Knowing these audiences is vital, and reacting appropriately is a key factor to an effective leader. Take a moment to answer these questions to reflect on qualities that deal with flexibility.

- Do you keep calm in the face of difficulties?
- Do you have physical symptoms of stress when you have to be flexible?
- Do you show signs of anger or frustration when told about a situation where you will ultimately have to be flexible?
- Do you think quickly and come up with ideas on how to change?
- Do you react quickly and take on challenges on a short notice?
- Do you try to plan ahead and can you foresee changes that you believe may be occurring?
- Can you cite examples of when you were flexible and the outcomes were positive?
- Can you cite examples of when you were not flexible and the outcomes were not positive?

Adaptability

Coping effectively with change equates with adaptability. Research suggests that one of the most important traits of an effective leader is adaptability. Being able to adapt is a strength that gives a competitive advantage to you and your organization. Accepting the change is one thing, being flexible to change is another, but adaptability means that you will continually grow and adapt to the situations as they evolve. This means that you are willing to change often and with purpose. Here are some reflective questions that can help you to see your comfort level in terms of being an adaptive leader:

- Are you an active, dynamic leader?
- What type of influence do you exert on others?

- Do you foresee the next step in the change before it is even needed?
- Can you come up with multiple ways to solve problems?
- Do you see your workforce as an evolving environment?
- Do you provide areas of growth even when there are not problems to tackle or changes that have to be made?
- Do you encourage growth and change in everyone?
- Do you focus on the activities or the outcomes?
- Are the roles and responsibilities of your faculty fluid?
- How is information shared?
- Are you willing to take risks?

Creativity

Some decisions will not always be so clearcut. You may be forced at times to deviate from your set course and make a decision "on the fly." This is where your creativity will prove to be vital. In the past, creativity was often considered to be fluff and not regarded as educational or meaningful as the facts. There is a distinct difference between quantitative and qualitative data. Some people only value the numbers or the facts and refuse to think about being innovative or creative. This will limit the ability to change effectively. Here are a few questions to reflect on your own views about being creative.

- Are you threatened by creativity?
- Do you feel comfortable with standards?
- Do you think outside the box?
- Do you welcome outside views?
- Do you encourage networking and collaboration?
- Can you generate creative ideas?
- Do you have a network and/or team of creative individuals?
- Do you encourage innovation?
- Do you value your faculty who have creative roles as much as those who have more of factual-driven roles? (This may be the English department or Math department vs. the Art or Language department.)

Key 13

Recognizing the qualities it takes to be flexible, adaptable, and creative is essential to being an effective leader. Changes will occur often and it is during these critical situations that your team will look to you for guidance. Do you have the qualities and skills necessary to be a leader who promotes growth and welcomes change? Do you lead an organization that is fluid and continually shows growth?

What the Experts Say

Taking risks to make changes can be challenging and pressure-filled. Having the skills and support to feel comfortable to take those risks is important. Following necessary plans and knowing when to deviate from those plans is vital to the success of the plans that were generated. Knowing the scope of the change, the timeframe, and the importance of the outcomes also are aspects that leaders need to know whenever changes occur.

Often in education there are challenges and tasks assigned that are not as concrete in regards to solving the problem. One of these that always seems to be a topic of focus is improving test scores. The solution is not that simple, but the pressure to succeed is immense.

Dr. Ann Hart, President of the University of Arizona, shares how novice leaders can deal with that pressure: "Pressure to make change is indeed uncomfortable, especially in organizations and institutions accustomed to social support rather than task orientation. If at all possible, one should find ways to articulate uncomfortable change as a contribution to the shared positive outcomes to which the group is committed, such as student success in the case of test scores."

Dr. Nancy Zimpher, the New York University Chancellor, shares the following in regards to handling pressure and taking risks:

> I am a proponent of the "Don't let perfect be the enemy of good" approach to driving change. You can't always wait for perfect. That leads to analysis paralysis. We need to try; we need to move. We need to experiment, take what seem to be the best, data-supported ideas out for a spin and see how they work, and discover from there, through practice, how and where we can do better. The ***StriveTogether*** approach to improving a range of student outcomes is a concrete example of how this philosophy works. Creating community stakeholder-driven collective impact frameworks takes, in addition to absolute dedication, flexibility

and adaptability on the parts of the participants. This isn't always easy. People are used to working in their silos, and stepping outside of silos to come around a table and work together in new ways really is the definition of flexibility and adaptability. These are learned behaviors for a lot of leaders; it doesn't always—or often—come naturally, especially to leaders who maybe got to where they are by grabbing the reins. But the collective impact approach to solving complex issues means everyone's got a hand on the reins. This is not business as usual.

Judy Vredenburgh, Director of Girls Inc., shares her thoughts on creativity and adaptability in respects to effective leadership. She also addresses how she has adapted to a changing culture as a CEO. She states that the capacity to provide creative solutions to novel problems can be important in some leadership roles: "Since change is constant in many sectors and industries, demonstrating an adaptive capability to changing conditions is often necessary for effective leadership." As CEO of two nonprofit organizations she has had to undertake cultural change twice, particularly emphasizing the values of performance measurement and goal orientation. She has included cultural change in her strategic planning process, led by example, and incorporated new values and norms in the performance appraisal system. She hires those who reflect the same desired values.

Changes occur on a global level, not just on a local scale. Schools, as well as businesses, have to recognize this change. With global travel, international programs, and curriculums that focus on international studies, we have to think globally, not just locally. We are not only looking at test scores within a school system; we are looking at competing against or even partnering with other nations. This grand scale of change can be overwhelming and intimidating, but it is necessary.

Emmanuel Gobillot, the author of *The Connected Leader* (UK), talks about change:

> I am not sure I would see either as any more important in the 21st century as in the past—we all tend to think about our times as experiencing unprecedented change but I do think the introduction of the steam engine caused as much disruption as the search engine did. The main difference is that we now know how little we know, as we are more aware of global advances. So the main change that plays on leadership is not the rate of change, but the global nature of it. We now need to operate in cultures we do not understand, which is why adaptability

and innovation are as key today as they ever were. Being able to adapt to the way things are done across the globe and get the best out of people of different cultures requires an innovative approach to leadership indeed (along with a great deal of intercultural competence).

"Be adaptable, nimble and know when to deviate from your plans to leverage new opportunities," is advice shared by Phyllis M. Wise, the Chancellor of the University of Illinois at Urbana-Champaign. She states that this is where the difference between a clear vision and a strategic plan becomes very important. The vision is the destination—the plan is just the best route at one point in time. There are going to be unexpected opportunities along the way: ones that are not in any plan and ones with very narrow windows of time. You have to be willing and ready to deviate from your plans or to rethink them to take advantage of these. And you have to make sure those on your team believe they have that same flexibility.

Ideas to Try

- **Test the *level* of your adaptability.** There are programs that can help you assess your own level of adaptability. Considering taking one of these assessments can help you to better understand your own qualities and strengths. StrengthsFinder or Emotional Competence Inventory (ECI) are programs that can help you learn about your own skills. StrengthsFinders helps you to learn your strengths as a leader. The ECI program looks at four scales of adaptability: openness to new idea, adaptation to situations, handling of unexpected demands, and adapting or changing strategy.

- **Does your *title* lead the way, or do *you*?** Do not expect people to follow you because of the title you hold. Think about how you communicate your information. Do you dictate? Do you lead the way by modeling or do you tell others what to do? "Because I said so" or "Because I am the boss" is not the reason why anyone should follow your plan or advice. Your title should give credence to your actions. Your followers like to know there is something to back up your plans, but that should not be the reason for dictating. In our school department, chairs are chosen by the qualities they possess, not only because of their accomplishments. We have many doctorates on staff who are not in leadership positions. It is not about the title, it is about the qualities the person possesses.

- **Pushing the envelope**. Learning to try nontraditional solutions, or approaching problems in nontraditional ways will help you to solve an otherwise unsolvable problem. Most employees will also be impressed and inspired by a leader who doesn't always choose the safe, conventional path. Don't be the administrator that always goes by the book. Be willing to throw that book out the window sometimes and take a creative path. This shows that you are willing to take risks. It may also give you the opportunity to include various different groups of people in decision-making. Remember: before you push the envelope, do your research and be sure that the risk is worth the reward.

- **Facilitator of change**. Be a part of the change in a positive and motivating way. This includes providing a clear vision, having the credentials to back up your plan, being persistent in achieving goals, communicating effectively, and being virtuous and respectful in the process. Lead by example and be an active part of the team.

- **Evolution and adaptation**. Be open to continual change. Problems or challenges are always evolving, and so should you. This is the *create and recreate* aspect of the leadership role. You will need to modify and adjust plans regularly. Be open to this idea. This may mean that you are giving up an idea that you may have bought into hook, line, and sinker. Be willing to give it up and move on. It is nothing personal. Evolution occurs for survival of the species. In order to survive, be willing to continually adapt.

- **Know your *team*?** You are only as strong as the weakest member of your team. Know the qualities your faculty and staff possess. This will help you to be able to recognize people that can help you deal with various changes as they occur. Also, this will assist you when hiring new people. You can look for specific qualities that will help make your team stronger. Here are some of the most sought-after traits of employees:

    o   showing willingness to learn new methods and grow professionally

    o   being proactive in looking for ways to solve problems and help others adjust to change

    o   being willing to take on new tasks or initiatives

    o   being self-reliant, positive, and having a can-do attitude

Key 13

- keeping an open mind, looking for a creative solution, and being willing to take risks
- being a respectful team member

- **Calculate risks**. Too often we react and are not proactive. Even if you have to make a quick decision, calculate the risks. Speaking off the cuff or making a rash decision can have more negative consequences than if you find a way to calculate the risks first. This may be thinking twice before you speak and doing a quick mental calculation, or it may mean conducting a major study. Whatever the situation, be sure to calculate the risks first.

- **Transcend ego**. Agile leaders naturally think less of "me" and more of "we," having long ago abandoned command-and-control power trips. Transactional leaders focus more on self, but servant and transformational leaders focus more on others.

Key Points to Remember: Being Flexible, Adaptable, and Creative

- Recognize the importance of being flexible in your current position.
- Know the strengths of your employees and team members, so they can help facilitate change.
- Be willing to adapt to change.
- Think creatively. Look for new ways to solve problems better.
- Be forward-focused. Looking down the road allows you to be less rigid in the moment.
- Transcend ego. Think of others first.

# Key 14 | Respond Effectively to Crisis

"True leadership will keep steady the course even in the worst of storms."
Brad Johnson

"Crisis" is not a term that we like to associate with schools, but unfortunately it has become a word that is used too often. A crisis can have many meanings. It is a stage in a sequence of events at which the trend of all future events is determined. It can be a condition of instability or danger leading to a decisive change. It can also be a dramatic emotional or circumstantial upheaval in a person's life (http://dictionary.reference.com/browse/crisis). There are many different situations that can qualify as a crisis; it is your role as a leader to identify the situations and execute plans that have already been designed.

How we respond to crisis is also important. Often when issues arise, we simply react to them. However, reacting is an unconscious process where we experience an emotional trigger, but responding is a conscious process that involves noticing how you feel, then deciding how you want to behave. Responding is part of heightened EQ and is important in handling crises. Therefore in this chapter we want to examine some of the crises that can occur and how best to respond to them in a conscious, thought-out manner.

Natural Disasters

Every state in the United States, as well as countries all over the world, experiences natural disasters. Natural disasters can create humanitarian disasters where the safety and health of a large group of people can be affected. Some come with advanced warnings, such as a hurricane or a forest fire, but others come with little or no warning at all, such as a tornado, tsunami, or earthquake. Knowing that natural disasters occur means that you can be proactive with this type of crisis. Each type of disaster has its own unique plan. There are drills that can be done and emergency plans that can be established. It is imperative that you do research and know the type of natural disaster that may occur in your area. It is also important that your plan includes regularly scheduled drill, including practice communication with community members. The crisis is not over when the event is over. That is usually when the emotional crisis continues. Depending on the type of disaster, the scope of the crisis may be very far-reaching. At times, national and international help can be available. Knowing your plan and having your resources in order will help to aid all involved in the crisis.

Traumatic Events

A traumatic event can be any type of event that impacts the population. It often is correlated with the death of a student or member of the school community. Each event is unique and has to be treated so. A suicide, a loss due to illness, a tragic car accident, or any other devastating situation, has its own set of events and should be treated as a crisis within the school. As a leader you should be ready for these situations to occur. While you hope it never happens, statistically it will at some point, in one form or another. For example, thousands of teens commit suicide each year; it is the third leading cause of death in the United States for 15- to 24-year-olds.

While it is hard to be proactive and prepare for such an event, there are steps that can be taken. First, are you proactive with the support in your school, such as with guidance counselors and programs to help troubled children? With the topic of suicide, it does not just happen as an accident. Studies show that at least 90% of teens that kill themselves have some type of health problem, such as depression, anxiety, behavior issues, abuse, or a struggle with sexual identity. Can you be proactive with the type of culture you have at your school? Do you promote tolerance? How do you deal with the topics of transgender or homosexuality? Do you have a team on hand to help? Do you have connections with the community for support? Are you willing to make changes, some atypical, to meet the needs of the school community you are leading? These are hard topics and you will have to make difficult choices, but you are the leader and have to go in with your eyes wide open to crises that can occur and know that some can possibly be avoided based on the decisions you make.

Violence in Our Schools

Bullies, drugs, weapons, fights, theft, bombs, gang violence, and threats are commonplace within our schools. Violence in schools is not a new problem, but it is becoming a crisis. Bullies cause physical and mental abuse. The drugs, theft, and fights in schools are a problem. According to the Centers for Disease Control and Prevention (CDC), the following facts from a 2011 national survey for Grades 9–12 can be used to help understand what is happening in our school in relation to violence and help with violence prevention:

- 12% reported being in a physical fight on school property in the 12 months before the survey.
- 5.9% reported that they did not go to school on one or more days in the 30 days before the survey because they felt unsafe at school or on their way to or from school.
- 5.4% reported carrying a weapon (gun, knife, or club) on school property on one or more days in the 30 days before the survey.
- 7.4% reported being threatened or injured with a weapon on school property one or more times in the 12 months before the survey.
- 20% reported being bullied on school property and 6% reported being bullied electronically during the 12 months before the survey.

There are documented cases of extreme violence, death, and crisis situations in schools all throughout history. Here are just a few instances shared by CNN:

- **May 18, 1927**—Bath Consolidated Schoolhouse, Michigan. Farmer Andrew Kehoe sets off two explosions at the school, killing himself, 6 adults, and 38 children.
- **September 15, 1959**—Edgar Allan Poe Elementary, Houston. Convict Paul Orgeron explodes a suitcase of dynamite on a school playground, killing himself, two adults and three children.

- **March 18, 1975**—Sumner High School, St. Louis. 16-year-old Stephen Goods, a bystander, is shot and killed during a fight between other teens.
- **February 24, 1984**—49th Street School, Los Angeles. Sniper Tyrone Mitchell shoots at children on an elementary school playground, killing 1 and injuring 11. He later takes his own life.
- **April 12, 1993**—Dartmouth High School, Massachusetts. 16-year-old Jason Robinson is stabbed to death in his social studies class by three teenage attackers who invade the classroom.
- **April 20, 1999**—Columbine High School, Littleton, Colorado. 18-year-old Eric Harris and 17-year-old Dylan Klebold kill 12 fellow students and 1 teacher before committing suicide in the school library.

The list goes on and on. The final one on the list, the crisis at Columbine High School, was one that rocked the nation. After looking into the details behind the attack, police found home videos referencing what they were going to do, as well as a police report filed by a parent for death threats to her child, along with death threats posted on the internet by one of the shooters. Could this have been prevented? That question can never truly be answered, but it is one worth pondering. Were the signs missed or ignored?

But even after Columbine, more shootings and violence have taken place. The one that broke hearts across the country and world was Sandy Hook Elementary. On December 14, 2012, Adam Lanza gunned down 20 children ages 6 and 7—and 6 adults, school staff, and faculty—before turning the gun on himself, making the total death count 27. These were innocent children. How as a leader would you cope with that type of tragedy and loss? How do you begin to even wrap your mind around something like that? It is sad that you would even have to, but you must, because since the Sandy Hook massacre CNN reports that there have been 74 school shootings in the 18 months that followed. In the United States there have been 13 school shootings recorded in the first six weeks of 2014 alone. Violence in schools is a crisis that as a leader you need to be prepared for.

Crisis Preparation is essential to being a successful leader. You need to think of all parties that can be impacted by the crisis, including yourself. If you cannot emotionally handle a situation, then you are in no position to lead. Pre-crisis job performance training is available. It would be wise to look into this and see what your district or state provides in regards to training. This will help with preparedness for emotional crisis and post-crisis stress. Emotions such as grief, sadness, and guilt can be associated with a crisis or traumatic event. Knowing the symptoms and countermeasures can be crucial when it comes to handling the situation effectively, both personally and professionally. Early treatment can lead to quicker recovery and minimize long-term damage. This is where resilience comes into play.

How do you as a leader help your school community bounce back from a crisis? How do you promote a culture of resilience? How do you help the social and emotional wellbeing of the school community after a devastating loss or event? How do you help them go on with their lives, because going on is what they must do, no matter how painful? Coping and functioning despite the adversity is resilience. Implementing a resilience training program can not only help in a crisis situation, but can also be carried over into other aspects of life. Being resilient means having the knowledge and skill to know how to proceed and persevere.

What the Experts Say

According to Emmanuel Gobillot, author of *The Connected Leader* (UK), leading in crisis probably deserves a book of its own but in the main to be equipped to deal with crisis means strong self-awareness and self-control. What derails most leaders in crisis is an overemphasis on prior perceived strength (if they were once good at selling, they will sell even more, for example) or a default to a preferred leadership style (directive, for example). This tends to be more unhelpful than helpful. First, great leaders remain calm in order to understand if it is indeed a crisis (few leaders actually experience real crisis in their career, in the same way as few pilots will ever experience an emergency landing). A lot of the situations we encounter are stressful, but they are not crises. To do this diagnosis, one must be aware of one's default positions and not be hijacked by them. I advise leaders to buy an egg timer and turn it when they feel they are in crisis. This should give them enough time to think things through without feeling they run the risk of being too slow!

Rachael Robertson, Antarctic Expedition Leader, leadership expert, author, speaker, and mentor, shares a crisis situation where she was the leader:

> In Antarctica I managed the search and rescue following a plane crash that stranded four of my people 500 kilometers away. A bolt had sheared

off the landing gear, so the plane couldn't taxi or take off. So the team was stranded until the weather cleared and we could send an aviation engineer out to fix the plane, several days later.

It taught me four important lessons about leading through a crisis:

- *Visibility*. Be seen about the place. It's natural to want to bunker down with your leadership team and manage the detail, but you need to be front and center. *It's not enough to be leading; you need to be seen to be leading.*
- *Verbal palette*. Choose your words with care: during the plane crash I spoke about retrieval, not a rescue. I had "concerns," but I wasn't "worried." Different words convey different messages.
- *Composure*. Make sure your body language mirrors your optimism. Be calm and poised. Carry yourself confidently and it will instill confidence in those around you.
- *Communicate*. All available information—all the time. If you don't send regular updates, people will fill in the gaps themselves, and often these "gap fillers" are worse than the reality.

Every leader will encounter a difficult period when things get tough. It may be a financial crisis, a natural disaster, or an emergency. For me, it was a plane crash. We're drilled on how to manage these events, but we often forget about the leadership role. The role of the leader remains the same, no matter what the crisis is. *It's not enough to be leading; you need to be seen to be leading.*

Gina Ikemoto, Executive Director of Research and Policy Development at New Leaders, shares her thoughts on leadership skills needed to handle a crisis in school:

Crisis in school, unfortunately, is pretty often. It is paramount that a leader stays calm and keeps a level head during crisis. Preparation for potential crisis is important as well. A leader needs to be aware of resources and be willing and able to tap them quickly. They must strategically work with policy, the public, and the community at large to decrease anxiety quickly. This requires socio-emotional intelligence and communication to help others understand and navigate crisis situations.

It also requires resilience in order to recognize "things will not always be this way" and that people can make a difference.

According to Child Trends' researchers, resilience training is vital to helping a school survive a crisis. Child Trends and their partners on the National Center for Safe and Supportive Learning Environments have compiled resources that can help schools to build resilience in their students (http://safesupportivelearning.ed.gov/hot-topics/response-and-resiliency). Looking across these resources, here are some strategies that schools can use to build resilience in students:

- Promote positive social connections between staff and students, among students, and between schools and home.
- Nurture positive qualities, such as empathy, optimism, or forgiveness, and give students a chance to use them.
- Notice and reinforce qualities that are key to resilience.
- Avoid focusing on failure or negative behaviors.
- Teach by example, which is an effective approach; train staff to develop the same qualities.
- Apply restorative justice techniques; these can help schools by giving students a structured opportunity to work difficulties out by encouraging reflection and empathy.
- Foster feelings of competence and self-efficacy.
- Set high expectations for students; teach them to set realistic, achievable goals, and also how to reach out for help when needed.

Ideas to Try

- **Identify possible crisis situations that can occur (natural and man-made).** What natural disasters have happened in your state? Knowing the possible chances for a natural disaster can help you be better prepared for a crisis. Do some research and find out the likelihood of a natural disaster. Be sure to have drills and create a plan.
- **Form teams.** Who are your go-to people who can help with support when needed? Do you have a crisis management team? What role does your guidance counselor play? Do you have connections with a

Key 14

chaplain? Is the local law enforcement a part of the team? What about parents, board members, or community members? What roles do the teachers, faculty, and staff play? What about the students—do they have any roles?

- **Generate site-specific emergency plans**. These plans should include specific guidelines for everyone involved, including plans for communication and seeking alternate shelter for safety. Two sites leaders in the US can use that can be helpful are: http://www.ready.gov/school-emergency-plans and http://www.ready.gov/kids

- **Create emergency kits**. Being proactive and having kits can really help in a crisis situation. There should be a kit for any type that could possibly occur. This may mean having water bottles available for classrooms or first-aid kits in central locations. After the kits are created, be sure to communicate where they are, how to use them, and when to use them.

- **Identify the victim, perpetrator, and bystander**. When a crisis situation occurs, it is important to know the role of the people in the crisis. Each role may require a different set of responses.

- **Professional development and training**. Training can help with preparedness for crisis situations. There is professional development for training plans, crisis management, resilience training, and more. Here are a few sources and sites that may help:

    - http://resiliencefirst.com/training.html

    - http://training.fema.gov/programs/emischool/emischool.aspx/el361toolkit/glossary.htm

    - http://www.childtrends.org/what-can-schools-do-to-build-resilience-in-their-students/

- **Don't ignore situations**. If a situation is reported to you, then it is deemed important by the reporter. Be sure to follow up and take appropriate measures, even if they are hard choices or actions to take. Reports of bullying cannot go ignored. Also be aware of social and cultural situations. Transgender and homosexuality are not rare occurrences. Racial tension is still prevalent. Don't be naïve. Events that happen outside of school often find their ways into the school setting. Be aware of situations and do not ignore any information that crosses your path.

- **Recognize adversity and know the risks.** Family problems, school problems, health issues, poverty, violence, peer rejection, and crises are all examples of types of adversity that can undermine a child's mental health and interfere with learning. Possible risks for children facing adversity are: academic failure, social maladjustment, health problems, poverty, mental illness, substance abuse, law enforcement involvement.

Key Points to Remember: Responding Effectively to Crisis

- A crisis can occur while you are leader.
- Know the types of situations that are prone to occur in your area, whether it is a natural disaster or gang violence.
- Be proactive and create teams and generate plans.
- Carry out the plans, and be prepared for possible long-term mental and emotional damage.
- Be supportive to yourself and others.
- In a crisis, remember to make a conscious response, not simply an emotional reaction.

Key 15 | Know When to Seek Help

"A leading expert was once a novice who simply wouldn't give up."
Brad Johnson

One fallacy of leadership is that the individual should know it all or be proficient in every area of leadership. This is an unrealistic and unfair expectation. People assume that you were hired for a job, so that means that you are qualified for that job. Well, being qualified does not mean that you have all of the answers all of the time. Again, that is an unrealistic and unfair expectation.

So, when do you ask for help? That is a tough question and one that often comes with different answers. The key is that you ask if you need it. Here are a few aspects broken down in a little more detail that can hopefully help you decide when to seek help.

Do You Know the Answer?

If you can answer a question with utmost certainty, then you do not need to seek help. If you don't know an answer, then decide what to do from here. You can either make your own educated guess or seek help. The importance of the question will help you to determine if you make your educated guess or if you ask others. Weigh your options carefully, because there could be consequences for asking or not asking.

Key 15

Can You Find the Answer?

If you can find the answer on your own, then go for it. Hopefully you will be working with a team in many aspects of your leadership position, so it is OK to go at it alone. Finding out information on your own can show perseverance and the ability to gather information. The key with this is to make sure when you try to find an answer that you are using reliable and credible sources.

Who Should You Ask for Help?

This depends on the question. Hopefully you will have a mentor or a collaborative group in which you will be working. Those would be your go-to people. With collaborative groups or with having a mentor, it would be easy and even expected to be asking questions and seeking advice and others' opinions. But what if you have to go outside that comfort zone and seek "outside" help? So what? Do it! The important thing now is to find the best person to ask. You may even have to go to multiple people to seek help. These people then just become a part of your already existent support group. Your group should continue to grow.

Can You Leave Your Ego Out of It?

Are you embarrassed if you do not know an answer? Can you admit you are wrong? Do you think you look like a failure if you can't solve a problem? Can you swallow your pride? Are you ashamed if you have to seek help? While these are normal feelings, they should not get in the way of solving whatever issue you have going on in which you need help. Being prideful is a common trait, but not one for a leader to showcase. You have to be willing to swallow your pride and ask for help.

Are You a Control Freak?

For you power-hungry people who have problems letting go of a little control, asking for help will be a challenge. By asking others for help, you are giving up your power to control the situation. The idea that someone else may be in control, if only for a short time, is often hard for some people to cope with. Pick and choose your battles. Can you give up something in order to see advances and improvements in the long run? Don't be so closed-minded, and instead look at the big picture. This will help make it a bit easier not always to be controlling over every aspect of your leadership position.

Have You Waited Too Long?

Waiting too long can cause huge issues. The problem can just grow and grow and possibly get larger than it ever should have been if you would only have asked earlier. Think of it like a weed: if you had addressed it in the first place, then it would be gone and you could move on to other weeds. When the situation arises where you may need some help, look at the timeframe of the issue. Weigh the pros and cons to asking right away or waiting. From there, make a decision on what to do in regards to seeking help.

Do You Ask Too Many Questions?

If you find yourself asking the same person over and over for help, then you need to ask yourself, and maybe even that person, if you are a bother. From there you need to do a little problem-solving. Do you ask the same person questions all of the time? Do you have enough people in your support group to go to for help? Are you really asking too many questions? Should you be taking care of more on your own? Are you really qualified for the leadership position you have? Some of these are serious questions and may take some soul-searching. But you have to know when to admit that you are doing yourself and others a disservice if you cannot adequately fill a leadership role you have been asked to do.

Have You Thought of Yourself as a Model?

When you ask others questions and seek help, it shows that you do not know everything. You model being humble and a team player. You are showing that you value others' opinions and thoughts. This will make others feel comfortable to follow suit.

Do You Need Extra Training?

Once they take over that position, how much training is a person in a leadership position given ? Truly, that depends on the position, but unfortunately it is rarely enough. In the business world, when people are hired to a corporation, they are usually immediately sent for training. This glaring flaw may be why there is such high turnover or attrition of teachers and administrators within the first three to five years of their career. If you were asked to be department chair, were you trained? If you were hired as principal, were you trained? Believe it or not, people are often put in leadership positions without formal training. Ask for training if you think you need it. This can only make you more comfortable in your new position.

Do You Know Your Policies?

There are times when you need to follow school, district, or state policies in regards to situations. Do you know them? Do you know when this needs to occur? Are there specific policies that you are mandated to follow and ones that you have say so over? You definitely need to know who to seek help from in these situations. Your job could be in danger, with possible legal ramifications if the policies are not followed.

Do You Know the Law?

While you are not expected to also hold a law degree, it is imperative that you are aware of lawful situations that can occur under your leadership. What alcohol or drugs are on campus? What if you find out child abuse has occurred? What if a teacher cheated on standardized tests? Do you know who to go to in order to seek legal advice for your school?

What the Experts Say

Kim Zilliox, leadership development expert, explained in our interview,

> I feel strongly about this one, based on years of anecdotal evidence. Great leaders are always looking to learn and improve. Great leaders

also respect other leaders who are looking to learn and improve. It is for this reason that asking for help is not actually considered weak, but is instead seen as a strength. The advice I have, though, is for young leaders to do everything in their power to learn on their own. This can include reading as many leadership books as they can, listening to Ted Talks, reading articles, and observing great leaders. They can also interview leaders to find out about what they have learned as leaders, what mistakes they have learned from, and keys to their success. One does not have to officially ask someone to be their mentor. A mentorship can be informal and look like quarterly lunches, coffees, or meetings where information is exchanged. Every single senior leader I have ever worked with enjoys mentoring younger leaders, either formally or informally. Just ask them!

Sally Helgesen, leadership and communication expert shared her ideas on seeking help by sharing:

> it's important to recognize that you need to seek help. You want to be clear about who you go to ... people who have the information or who have your back. These people need to be trustworthy, so it's important to make good choices. Then go to them, you can seek help while keeping your dignity intact.
>
> Some novice leaders will share every problem with their mentor, while others try to create the illusion that they are in control when they really aren't, and both of these situations can be dangerous.
>
> When seeking help, be very specific with a request to get advice, feedback, etc. Instead of feeling overwhelmed, be specific, such as in meetings this seems to occur, and I am not sure how to handle it. If you're specific, the more targeted the help can be, and being specific, the person helping understands you aren't just dumping on them, but respect their time and talent.
>
> Mentoring today seems to be novice leaders seeking too much help, or hand-holding, and then not heeding the advice of their mentors, although some young leaders feel like they don't need any help because they are in a leadership role. We have overstuffed the role of mentors.
>
> Young people also seem like to feel that the whole job of becoming successful is finding the right mentor or sponsor. They need self-awareness to examine what they really need to be successful.

Key 15

This can be done with conversations with peers, not just their own leaders.

Education tries to be inclusive and doesn't see business as applying to education, but leadership can be gleaned from different fields. Especially with technology and other constant changes, you can't be expected to be an expert in everything, so it's OK to ask for help. We don't know it all.

Fawn Germer, leadership expert, shared her insight on seeking help as a leader. She explained:

Well, think about it. How much do you respect people who don't know what they are doing, yet pretend that they do? Sure, you'd rather know everything you need to know, but this world moves too fast to know everything. A leader knows who to go to for help—and does it before the problem gets worse. I interviewed Meg Whitman back when she was the CEO of eBay and she told me that she arrived there with a second-grade computer proficiency. She knew business. She knew leadership. But she had to admit she knew nothing about the business she was driving. Now look at eBay.

Phyllis Wise, University of Illinois Urbana-Champlain Chancellor, explained that we should:

Find people who are willing to mentor you. And I have to say when I realized that people were willing to mentor me, and I started to actively ask questions it was very rare that someone would tell me that they didn't have the time. Most of the time, people are more than happy to give you advice; they are more than happy to tell you their stories; they are more than happy to mentor you.

And as you seek this kind of mentoring from multiple people, you will realize that many times you cannot follow all of the advice. Sometimes it's just not you, and what you have to do first and foremost is be able to live in your own skin. So, by seeking advice from a variety of people at a variety of times in their own careers, you will be able to get a repertoire that you will be able to pick and choose from. Sometimes advice is not appropriate for one decision, but maybe it becomes appropriate for the next decision.

Jim Kouzes explained:

Early in my career, I had the opportunity to interview Don Bennett, the first amputee to climb Mount Rainier. That's 14,400 feet on one leg and two crutches—an amazing achievement. I asked Don, "What is the most important lesson you learned in climbing that mountain?" Without hesitation Don responded, "You can't do it alone." I remind myself of that every day, and it's the advice I give all young leaders. It's advice I wish I'd gotten earlier in my career. No leader ever got anything extraordinary done without the talent and support of others. Not one. While we tend to make heroes out of individual leaders, the best leaders know that leadership requires teamwork and trust. As a leader you are only as strong as your team. You need others and they need you. You're all in this together. You have to be sensitive to the needs of others, listen, ask questions, develop others, provide support, and ask for help.

Ideas to Try

- **Ask questions**. Your employees are a never-ending source of ideas, many of which you may have never thought of or considered. When you ask them what they think, you're letting them know that you want and value their ideas.
- **Admit mistakes**. No employee respects a boss who refuses to admit making a mistake, or who tries to blame his or her own mistakes on a member of the team. Earn the respect of your people by quickly and publicly owning up to your mistakes, and then doing whatever it takes to correct them. And not only admit you're wrong, but apologize if necessary. This shows a personal connection and sincerity that your staff will respect.
- **Know your limits**. As a leader you want to be seen as competent. But with constant advances in science, technology and a global economy, no one knows it all. Effective leaders don't try to oversell themselves. They know their limits.
- **Find a mentor**. This can be a leader in the field, an experienced colleague, or even just a trusted friend. Meet with them on a regular basis if possible and make sure your mentor feels like you value their time and responses.
- **Be emotionally aware**. Becoming in tune with your responses to situations, increasing your self-awareness, and improving your relationships with your staff will greatly improve your effectiveness as a leader.

- **Learn from the past**. As you gain experience in your leadership role, don't forget the valuable lessons you learn from every situation. Reflect upon these and use those experiences when you face future issues.
- **Listen first, talk second**. This is an oft-underutilized skill among leaders. One key to being viewed as a respected leader is to actively listen to your staff/parents/students and then provide guidance and answers. Show people you care and respect them by actively listening and then responding.
- **Join a mentoring group**. Vistage is an organization that groups CEOs together in cities across the US. They meet regularly and act as mentors, support, and problem-solvers for each other. Educators could benefit from this type of group mentoring.

Key Points to Remember: Knowing When to Seek Help

- Never give up. If you want something bad enough, endure until you succeed.
- Create or join a mentoring group, such as Vistage.
- Build up those you lead, and lead them with integrity.
- Be forward-thinking.
- Focus on your strengths for maximum success.
- Work with your peers. Increase interaction with those in similar roles.
- Surround yourself with great employees.
- Listen twice as much as you speak.

Epilogue

Because we had access to some of the world's top leaders in fields such as education, business, and communication, we took the opportunity to ask some of them the following question:

> If you could go back in time and give a younger "you" one piece of advice, what would it be and why?

We wanted to leave you with the words of wisdom from these highly effective leadership experts.

Mike Abrashoff I would tell myself to work better with my peers. I give myself an A for working up and down the chain of command, but I give myself an F on peer-to-peer relationships.

Chester Elton I think I would take more chances, and not be afraid to do more on my own. Since leaving the structured world of larger companies about four years ago, I have had so many amazing experiences. I have had the chance to get involved in so many more businesses. To take an equity stake in those companies and to really expand my work life experiences. Things that just aren't possible when you are working 8:00 a.m. to 7:00 p.m. every day for a large company.

Arthur Carmazzi I would observe and say nothing, my mistakes have shaped me and taught me lessons, some hard and painful ones. But if my path had been easier, I would not have learned what I needed to learn or become what I needed to become. For a novice leader, I would say, try everything and fail, and when others in your greater future fail beneath you, remember what it was that made you great!

Marshall Goldsmith My advice would be simple. Figure out what makes you happy and what is meaningful for you. To have a great life, you need to find both happiness and meaning in what you are doing. If what you are doing is meaningful, but does not make you happy, you might be a great leader but you will not have a great life. You will be a martyr. In the long term, your misery will catch up with you. If what you are doing makes you happy, but is not meaningful, you might enjoy the "perks" of being a leader but you will not have a great life. You will be "amusing yourself to death." In the long term your emptiness will catch up with you. If you are doing what makes you happy and it is meaningful for you, you can be a great leader, who has a great life. These answers can only come from inside your heart. No one can define happiness and meaning for you but you!

Dianna Booher Surround yourself with the best leaders you can find, and don't be afraid to be vulnerable and honest about what you don't know. Ask questions—particularly "why" questions. Learn how the best leaders think and what questions they ask themselves to guide their decision-making. Those who ask the best questions make the best strategic decisions. Inexperienced leaders frequently hide their weaknesses; thus, they lengthen their path to mastery.

John Baldoni As for advice … what my father taught me about persistence holds true. If you want something bad enough, go for it. Don't worry about the obstacles. You can chip them away, or go around them. I learned that as a 15-year-old applying for my first job as a gardener's assistant. The lesson rings true today.

As for what I might counsel a younger self, it would be the value of patience. Learn to accept life as it comes. You do not control circumstances. You control your reaction to circumstances.

Sally Helgesen Trust the ideas you come up with. I had good ideas but abandoned them as soon as I was given pushback on them. But I also wish I would have given more thought to how I articulated my ideas and vision.

Christina Parker I have learned so much over the years … being a leader doesn't mean that you have to have all of the answers. It means that you have to select, develop, and invest in those around you that are stronger than you in areas, so that collectively you can come up with good solutions/answers. Being a leader means that you lead others by looking through their eyes. Leaders focus on the results more than the activities—focusing on doing the right things, what is truly important. Good leaders are more character-driven people versus emotion-driven people.

Rachael Robertson If you want something, ask for it. Don't sit around hoping someone will notice and offer it to you. They won't. So go out and get it yourself. Many future leaders hold themselves back simply because they don't ask for what they want. We assume that if we work really hard, deliver projects on time and on budget, then we'll get noticed and eventually get promoted. That might happen but it might not. In my first job I had a fantastic colleague who later became a mentor to me. One day in conversation I said to him, "I wish I could do your job when you go on annual leave." I just wanted a bit of a change, but without any real drastic commitment, and two weeks acting in a different role sounded like fun. He said to me, "Well, why don't you? Why don't you ask the boss?" I was stunned and thought, "There's no way I could be that bold." But I did it and to my surprise not only was the boss happy for me to have a go in the new role for a few weeks, but he was grateful that someone had put their hand up to do the job. He'd been wondering how he would fill the absence and I'd given him a solution. Often our fear of rejection gets in the way, but this story taught me early on that if I don't ask, I probably won't receive.

Mike Krzyzewski (Duke Head Basketball Coach) The best advice that I would give a younger me would be to keep learning and keep adapting. Stay entrenched in a great value system while you are learning more about leadership and the people you are leading.

Mark Strom As a CEO, I would say, very few things are as urgent as they seem. The more quietly you go about change, the more deeply you will hear and admire people, and the more lasting any change will be.

Sam Silverstein It's not about what you get, but it's about what you give. You may end up giving a lot, but you will also get a lot.

Phyllis Wise Realize that the path may change. I can say with complete authority that "Be the top administrator at a major public research university" was never on my childhood list of things to do. Years ago, when I earned my doctorate and started my academic career, my goal was to understand the molecular biology and biochemistry of the brain and how the endocrine system influences the way the brain works, not to be a department head, a dean, or a provost. Yet, in the course of my career, I found myself in all of these roles. For me, my road to Illinois was in some significant ways an accidental path to a place I never envisioned. I have the privilege of representing the students, faculty, staff, and alumni of a university that can honestly claim to have changed our world. It may not have been where I ever expected to be, but for me it has turned out to be exactly where I am privileged to be.

Jim Kouzes I'd share one other bit of advice: focus on the future. Focusing on the future sets leaders apart. In our research, Barry Posner and I have found that the skill that sets leaders apart from individual contributors is their ability to be forward-looking. It's the distinguishing leadership practice. It's also the skill that's the toughest to master—especially for younger leaders. We find in our research that college students, for example, value being forward-looking less than more experienced leaders. There are so many immediate priorities that can steal your time and attention away from looking to the future. But to become an exemplary leader you have to spend more time, not less, reflecting on the forces that are shaping people's lives 5, 10, even 25, years out. You have to understand other people's hopes, dreams, and aspirations. You need to build consensus around a shared vision of the future. You need to express your enthusiasm for the exciting possibilities ahead.

Remember that these highly effective leadership experts didn't have all the answers in the beginning; they were novices who learned to develop and grow as leaders. In the same way, you can develop and grow in your role as a school leader to become more effective and more inspirational to your staff. Best of luck on your journey!

Sources

Akers, M. & Porter, G. (2007). What is Emotional Intelligence (EQ)? Psych Central. Retrieved from www.fastcompany.com/3026707/work-smart/5-ways-to-boost-your-emotional-intelligence

Allison, E. (2011/2012) The resilient leader. December 2011/January 2012. *Resourceful School*, 69(4): 79–82. Retrieved from www.ascd.org/publications/educational-leadership/dec11/vol69/num04/The-Resilient-Leader.aspx

Avolio, B. J., & Bass, B. M. (2002). *Developing Potential Across a Full Range of Leadership: Cases on Transactional and Transformational Leadership*. Mahwah, NJ: Lawrence Erlbaum Associates.

Avolio, B. J., Bass, B. M., & Young, D. (1999). Re-examining the components of transformational and transactional leadership using the multifactor leadership questionnaire. *Journal of Occupational and Organizational Psychology*, 72: 441–462.

Bass, B. M. (1990). From transactional to transformational leadership: Learning to share the vision. *Organizational Dynamics*, 18: 19–31.

Bass, B. M. (1995). Transformational leadership: Looking at other possible antecedents and consequences. *Journal of Management Inquiry*, 4, 293–297.

Bass, B. M., & Riggio, R. E. (2006). *Transformational Leadership* (2nd ed.). Mahwah, NJ: Lawrence Erlbaum Associates.

Bennis, W. (2009). *On Becoming Leaders*. New York: Basic Books.

Black, D. (2013). *The Leadership Mandate: 10 Essential Elements to Developing the Leader Within You*. [Ebook]. Available at http://www.amazon.com/The-Leadership-Mandate-Dan-Black-ebook/dp/B00FE81ASO

Cherry, K. (n.d.). What is transformational leadership? *About.com Psychology*, Retrieved from http://psychology.about.com/od/leadership/a/transformational.htm

Folkman, J. and Zenger, J. (2012). *How to Be Exceptional: Drive Leadership Success by Magnifying Your Strengths*. New York: McGraw-Hill.

Groysberg, B. & Abrahams, R. (2014). Manage your work, manage your life. *Harvard Business Review*. Retrieved from https://hbr.org/2014/03/manage-your-work-manage-your-life

Hargis, Michael B., Wyatt, John D., & Piotrowski, C. (2011). Developing leaders: Examining the role of transactional and transformational leadership across contexts business. *Organization Development Journal*, 29(3): 51–66.

Hay, I. (2006). Transformational leadership: Characteristics and criticisms. Retrieved September 2, 2013 from https://hbr.org/2014/03/manage-your-work-manage-your-life

Kohlberg, L. (1975). The cognitive-developmental approach to moral education. *Phi Delta Kappan*, 56(10): 670–677.

Lynch, M. (2012). *A Guide to Effective School Leadership Theories* (1st ed.). New York: Routledge.

Onorato, M. (2013). Transformational leadership style in the educational sector. *Academy of Educational Leadership Journal*, 17(1): 33–47.

Online Sources

http://helpguide.org/mental/eq5_raising_emotional_intelligence.htm

http://resiliencefirst.com/index.html

http://resiliencefirst.com/resilience_quotes.html

http://training.fema.gov/programs/emischool/emischool.aspx/el361toolkit/glossary.htm

www.cdc.gov/violenceprevention/pdf/school_violence_fact_sheet-a.pdf

www.childtrends.org/what-can-schools-do-to-build-resilience-in-their-students/

www.cnn.com/2013/09/19/us/u-s-school-violence-fast-facts/

www.cnn.com/2014/06/11/us/school-shootings-cnn-number/

Sources

www.edutopia.org/resilience-grit-resources

www.elephantjournal.com/2013/01/10-quotes-to-inspire-your-inner-voice-rebecca-schwarz/

www.forbes.com/sites/joefolkman/2014/01/30/in-2014-are-you-fixing-your-weakness-or-building-your-strength-heres-what-matters-most/

www.healthychildren.org/English/health-issues/conditions/emotional-problems/Pages/Teen-Suicide-Statistics.aspx

www.mindtools.com/CommSkll/ActiveListening.htm

www.nctsn.org/resources/audiences/school-personnel/crisis-situation

www.psychologytoday.com/blog/your-mind-your-body/201201/10-ways-enhance-your-emotional-intelligence

www.prdaily.com/Main/Articles/Listening_facts_you_never_knew_14645.aspx

www.radicati.com/wp/wp-content/uploads/2013/04/Email-Statistics-Report-2013-2017-Executive-Summary.pdf

www.safeschools.info/docman/search_result

www.theguardian.com/world/2014/feb/12/school-shootings-newtown-study-gun-violence

www.worklifebalance.com/